Post Pathology

A NEW ORIENTATION TO MENTAL HEALTH

AF706126

Dr. Tiffany Ryan

SYNERGY
PUBLISHING GROUP
BELMONT, NORTH CAROLINA

Post Pathology: A New Orientation to Mental Health, the Human Experience Labyrinth

Dr. Tiffany Ryan

Copyright ©2026 Tiffany Ryan. All rights reserved. No portion of this book may be reproduced in any form without permission from the author, except as permitted by U.S. copyright law. Contact the author at dr.tiffanyryan@gmail.com.

Published by Synergy Publishing Group, Belmont, NC
Formatting by Melisa Graham

Softcover, June 2026, ISBN 978-1-960892-76-8
Ebook, June 2026, ISBN 978-1-960892-77-5

This book and overarching framework are a culmination of a lifelong journey to understand the meaning of life. Every person, every event, every trauma, every accomplishment, and every rejection in my life led me to this work. This is the contribution that my soul came here to offer in partnership with and inspired by Noah Jack Ryan. It is the meaning that allows me to be the strongest, softest, and highest version of myself for my Earthside children, Grant and Hope. Thank you. I love you.

Contents

SECTION I:

An Overview of the Current Reality

Introduction

"He who has a why to live for can bear with almost any how."
—Friedrich Nietzsche[1]

This book serves as a gentle wake up call—a reckoning with our current paradigm and a reorientation toward not just mental and emotional wellness, but life itself. Western society has largely come to define the role of mental health care as helping people feel better as quickly as possible. The goal is happiness or, at the very least, less suffering. And in many cases, we have become willing to achieve that relief even if it means disconnecting from, or numbing, our lived realities.

Viktor Frankl, a psychiatrist, neurologist, and Holocaust survivor, offered a fundamentally different orientation. His work on meaning-making provides a foundation for what I describe as the Human Experience Labyrinth—a framework for understanding and normalizing life in all of its complexity and depth. As Edith Weisskopf-Joelson observed in her reflections on Frankl's work, our cultural emphasis on happiness may, in fact, deepen suffering: "The burden of unavoidable unhappiness is increased by unhappiness about being unhappy."[2] In this way, individuals are not only experiencing pain, but are also taught, implicitly and explicitly, that this pain is something to be ashamed of and that working through suffering holds dignity.

From this foundation, I propose a shift in orientation. Rather than centering our lives around the pursuit of happiness, we might instead orient toward meaning and growth. The role of helping professionals, and of communities more broadly, is not simply to alleviate distress, but to help individuals understand the nature of the human experience, to create opportunities to fully engage with it, and to support one another in discovering meaning—their *why*. It is this sense of *why* that allows us to move through life's challenges again and again with some degree of coherence and purpose, even when the path feels unclear.

The metaphor of the Labyrinth offers a way to understand this process. Unlike a maze, which is designed to confuse and trap, a Labyrinth contains a single winding path. It moves inward and outward, at times bringing us closer to the center before leading us away again. From the outside, it may appear disordered or chaotic, but in reality, it is structured and purposeful. When we begin to view life through this lens, we can start to understand that the moments of difficulty, disorientation, and struggle are not deviations from the path, but part of it. When meaning is present, even profound hardship can be endured. When it is absent, even manageable challenges can begin to feel insurmountable.

This is why it becomes so important to normalize the Human Experience Labyrinth as a nonlinear, ever-evolving journey—one that inherently includes both heartbreak and joy, despair and hope. When we understand this, we are better able to hold the full range of experience without immediately seeking to escape it. Instead of viewing suffering as something that must be eliminated, we begin to see it as something that can be engaged with, understood, and, at times, transformed. There is a kind of beauty in this fuller participation in life, even when it is difficult—a sense of being connected to something larger than the immediate moment.

While many mental health interventions are designed to help people know how to feel better or manage challenging times, that relief is often temporary or tied to a specific outcome. Meaning, by contrast, is not something that can be given externally or applied as a technique. It is something that must be discovered and lived. As Frankl wrote, this meaning is unique and specific to each individual and "must be fulfilled by him alone; only then does it achieve a significance which will satisfy his own will to meaning."[3] This points to a deeper kind of work, one that is internal, eternal, and cannot be outsourced.

This raises an important question: How do we cultivate the kind of wisdom that allows individuals, families, and communities to move through suffering with greater capacity and understanding?

The answer is not found solely in education or intervention, but in embodiment. Wisdom is taught through the way we live, through the ways we show up for one another, and through the environments we create. It is modeled in homes, schools, workplaces, and communities, not as something abstract, but as something lived and witnessed. Our communities are in need of what might be called wise elders—not necessarily defined by age, but by their willingness to engage deeply with life and to share what they have learned in ways that are accessible and grounded.

If we want to support those around us, our children, our friends, and our communities, it begins with the work we are willing to do within ourselves. This is not work that can be outsourced to systems, even though those systems can play an important role. Therapy, education, and structured supports are valuable, but they are not sufficient on their own. Over time, we have come to rely heavily on formalized systems to address suffering and, in doing so, we have lost sight of our role within the broader ecosystem of human life. There is a difference between learning about something and living it. Both are necessary, but without integration into daily life, learning alone does not transform us.

When meaning is absent, it is natural that we turn toward comfort and pleasure as substitutes. We seek relief wherever we can find it. But when comfort becomes the primary goal, life's inevitable challenges begin to feel intolerable. Meaning, on the other hand, allows us to remain engaged even when things are difficult. It provides a kind of internal orientation that is not dependent on circumstances being easy or predictable.

Part of the difficulty lies in how often we approach these questions through an either/or lens. We ask whether we should reduce suffering or allow space for it, whether we should intervene or step back. In reality, both are necessary. There are times when suffering must be reduced—when it becomes overwhelming, when safety is at risk, when immediate support is needed. At the same time, when our entire framework is built around eliminating discomfort, we lose access to the deeper layers of experience that allow for growth and understanding. The Human Experience Labyrinth offers a way of holding both of these truths at once, helping us to orient toward meaning while still responding to immediate needs.

My Why

The day after my son died from consuming a full bottle of his antidepressant, Wellbutrin, I found myself sitting with a single, undeniable realization: I had to do something. To understand what had happened and remain silent felt impossible. A responsibility came with what I knew, both from my personal experience as a mother and from my professional background.

I am uniquely positioned to speak to this—both personally and professionally. With a PhD in social work, training in somatic practices, and experience building a wellness organization, I understand how individual, community, and systemic factors intersect. What became clear to me was that my son's death was not the result of a single factor, but rather a convergence—a "perfect storm" shaped by disconnection, societal pressures, medication effects, stigma, and a system that struggled to hold the full complexity of the human experience.

In the aftermath, I was met with an intensity of emotion that was difficult to put into words. There was rage, grief, and a profound sense of powerlessness. At times, it felt as though the weight of it might consume me. In order to survive, I had to step back from trying to understand everything at once and instead turn inward, focusing on my own process of healing and meaning-making.

Through that process, I came to recognize something that continues to shape how I understand this work: While we may not have control over many of the circumstances we face, we do have influence, particularly through the ways we choose to engage with our own lives. That influence becomes most powerful when it is embodied, when it is lived rather than simply understood. When we do the work of understanding ourselves, when we move through life with presence, authenticity, vulnerability, and intention, we give others permission and inspiration to do the same.

Systems Are Made Up of Individual Humans

Tackling systems reform and societal paradigm shifts can feel overwhelming. However, as your own internal perspective shifts from comfort to meaning, you may begin to see that many of our current systems, while well-intentioned, are missing something essential. Perhaps a systemic paradigm shift is needed. One that moves away from pathologizing the struggle of students, employees, patients, etc., and toward normalizing it as part of being human. Systems are operating in the same mindset that individuals have been—that suffering means something is wrong. So we seek to offer quick relief.

What if systems approached struggle differently?

What if we saw it as an opportunity for growth, reflection, and meaning-making?

Each of us becomes part of a ripple effect. The more we are willing to engage with ourselves honestly and deeply, the more we create conditions that allow others to do the same. As we have more understanding for where we are in the Human Experience Labyrinth, we can offer more grace and understanding to others who are in different layers of the Labyrinth. Whether as parents, practitioners, educators, or community members, the change we hope to see in the world begins with the ways we show up in our own lives and relationships.

It starts with you. It starts with the influence you have in your own internal world, in your family, in your workplace, and in your community.

It's time for a new way. We are in a new era of **Post Pathology: A New Orientation to Mental Health**. An era where we move from *Why me?* to *Why?* to *My Why.* As we move through the Human

Experience Labyrinth (HEL), it can feel like Hell when we are stuck in the *Why me*? As we realize that painful experiences happen to everybody, we begin to question, *Why does any of this happen to any of us*? The broader *why*. And as we find our way toward the center of the Labyrinth, we understand how every experience has shaped us to know our individual meaning, our purpose, our contribution—our own, unique *why*.

Suffering and pain are different animals. Pain is inevitable. Suffering—the prolonged experience of pain and resistance to our realities—is not. Our suffering often comes not from our experiences in and of themselves (though they are very well painful), but rather reliving the past, or the stories we tell ourselves about the future. It comes from our expectations of what should or should not happen. When we realize that our divorce, death, house fire, job loss, injury, etc., is a normal part of our human experience, the resistance to its existence fades. When the resistance fades, we can find an openness that allows for all types of experiences to exist. And when we can see the experiences in the larger framework of our movement toward meaning, we can find even greater peace.

This book is not meant to dismantle the field of mental health care; it is here to remind the field, and all of the systems that interact with humans, of what they have forgotten: to reorient individuals, those in the helping professions, and leaders in organizations and institutions from seeking immediate relief to holding a deeper container and meaning for the human experience.

This is suicide prevention. This is mental health care.

Let our love for our children and communities spur us toward self-discovery.

CHAPTER 1:

Beyond Diagnosis

Embracing the Messiness of the Human Experience

"You can't stop the waves, but you can learn to surf."
—Dr. Jon Kabat-Zinn, *Wherever You Go, There You Are*[4]

The mental health field has made meaningful progress in its efforts to understand and respond to human suffering. Over time, we have developed language, frameworks, and interventions that allow us to identify patterns of distress, offer treatment, and expand access to care. Diagnosis, in particular, has become a central organizing principle within modern systems, shaping clinical training, research, service delivery, and reimbursement. It has played an important role in bringing visibility and legitimacy to mental health within public health conversations.

Yet despite these advancements, something remains unresolved.

Rates of anxiety, depression, and suicidality continue to rise, even as access to treatment expands. More people are engaging with mental health services than ever before, yet many still feel unseen, misunderstood, or unchanged in any lasting way. This does not suggest the system is failing entirely, but rather invites us to examine the assumptions underlying how we define and respond to distress.

Diagnosis functions as a form of shorthand—categorizing complex human experiences into patterns that can be communicated and treated within large systems. This is particularly valuable in acute situations where clarity and coordination are essential. However, what is gained in efficiency is often not matched by depth. Diagnostic categories describe symptoms, but they do not fully capture the context in which those symptoms arise—personal history, relational dynamics, cultural influences, and existential questions.

People do not enter care as diagnoses. They come as individuals navigating loss, transition, trauma, identity shifts, and the demands of complex social environments. These experiences rarely fit neatly within diagnostic boundaries and, when filtered primarily through that lens, essential aspects of human experience can be overlooked, not out of neglect, but as a consequence of how systems are structured.

Within policy and institutional settings, there are strong incentives to prioritize what can be measured—symptom reduction, treatment adherence, and efficiency. These metrics serve an important purpose, particularly for accountability and scalability, but they can narrow the scope of care by emphasizing short-term stabilization over long-term understanding. In practice, this can look like prioritizing interventions that produce visible, measurable outcomes, while the deeper work of fostering connection, meaning, and humanity remains less resourced and harder to quantify.

This reflects a broader historical context. Many structures shaping modern mental health care emerged alongside industrialization, where efficiency, productivity, and scalability became dominant values. As care expanded into larger institutions, standardization became necessary. With this increased accessibility, it also introduced limitations—human experience does not unfold according to standardized timelines or protocols.

In this environment, agency can quietly erode. Care begins to feel like something done to individuals rather than developed with them. Clinicians, educators, and physicians often feel this tension as well. Many enter helping professions to support people in navigating life's complexity, yet institutional demands frequently prioritize documentation, metrics, and efficiency over relational depth. Over time, this contributes to moral distress and burnout.

Cultural misalignment further complicates this landscape. Diagnostic frameworks developed within Western psychiatric traditions do not always translate across contexts. In many communities, distress is understood through relational, spiritual, or communal narratives that differ significantly from medicalized models.

As a result, we find ourselves in a complex position: Systems designed to support well-being can also contribute to the conditions that undermine it. Social structures emphasizing productivity, individual responsibility, and constant performance create environments where disconnection, stress, and exhaustion are common. In response, interventions often focus on helping individuals cope so they can continue functioning within those same environments.

This is not a critique of any single component, but a recognition of how individual, community, and systemic layers interact to shape both suffering and our responses to it. From a social work perspective, the concept of "person in environment"[5] has long emphasized this interconnectedness. What remains less integrated is the extent to which those environments themselves require examination and, at times, transformation. When distress is understood only at the individual level, broader contributing conditions remain unaddressed.

This is where the gap between treatment and integration becomes most apparent. Access to care is essential, but it does not ensure that individuals can make sense of their experiences, reconnect with themselves or others, or develop sustained meaning. Treatment can alleviate symptoms, but it does not automatically lead to integration—the process of understanding, incorporating, and growing from experience.

Without integration, people often return to care repeatedly—finding relief that is real but temporary. The system responds as designed, yet underlying questions persist:

- Why is this happening?
- What does it mean?
- How do I move forward in a way that feels resourced and growth-oriented?

These are not questions that diagnosis alone can answer. They require a broader orientation—one that situates clinical tools within a more expansive understanding of human experience. What we are facing may not be a lack of treatment, but a limitation in how we conceptualize what it means to be human. We are at a crossroads. We have built systems that contribute to suffering—and then attempt to manage that suffering through coping and symptom reduction.

So what do we do?

We take a multi-level approach:

- Support individuals in the moment
- Strengthen communities
- Shift systems over time

In Section 3, practical recommendations are offered for individuals, helping professionals, and institutions. For this new orientation to take hold, it must be integrative—lived personally, practiced relationally, and embedded within systems.

Holding Two Truths at Once

Holding two truths at once, that we can and should reduce suffering and that discomfort is an essential part of being human, requires a shift in how we understand experience itself. An element of Taoism, the concept of Yin Yang offers a helpful lens. It reminds us that opposites are not problems to solve, but forces that define one another. Light has no meaning without darkness, just as joy has no depth without sorrow. When we strive for a life of only ease or happiness, we are not moving toward wholeness, we are denying half of reality.

Human experience is dynamic and interdependent. Within every moment exists the seed of its opposite. At any given time, we can feel joy and sorrow, hope and despair, longing and acceptance, etc. When we attempt to eliminate discomfort entirely, we often create imbalance. What is resisted does not disappear; it intensifies beneath the surface. Rather than striving for permanent relief, this perspective invites us into harmony. The goal is not to escape pain, but to move with it, reducing suffering when it becomes overwhelming, while allowing space for the natural cycles of growth and integration. This is where non-striving becomes essential. Trying to feel only good often creates more tension. Instead, we are invited to trust the process and engage with both light and shadow as necessary parts of becoming.

Holding two truths means recognizing that care requires both action and allowance. We intervene when suffering becomes too great, and we also make space for what cannot, and should not, be rushed. Accepting the messiness of transformation does not mean abandoning care. When distress becomes overwhelming or life-threatening, immediate relief is essential. Clinical interventions can be life-saving.

But relief alone cannot carry the full weight of the human journey. Once stability is restored, the deeper work begins: integration, meaning-making, and rebuilding one's relationship with self, others, and the world. The challenge is not choosing between treatment and meaning. It is learning to hold both.

A Shift in Orientation

This is where a post pathology orientation becomes useful. Post pathology does not reject clinical knowledge, diagnosis, or evidence-based care. These tools remain essential, particularly in moments of acute distress. Rather, post pathology shifts the primary orientation of care systems. Instead of asking only *how to correct pathology*, the question becomes, *How do we help people navigate the full complexity of the human experience?*

The Human Experience Labyrinth Overview

The Human Experience Is Not Linear

One of the greatest misunderstandings in modern approaches to mental health is the belief that human development should move in a clean, linear progression, from suffering to resolution. In reality, human life rarely unfolds this way. Periods of confusion, grief, doubt, and emotional upheaval are not anomalies in an otherwise stable system. They are part of the terrain of being alive. Transformation from suffering to growth and meaning-making is never tidy.

There are moments when identity dissolves before something new can take shape. Times when familiar beliefs no longer hold. Periods when individuals must sit in uncertainty, not knowing what comes next. Modern systems often interpret these moments primarily as problems to solve. But many spiritual traditions, psychological frameworks, and cultural practices throughout history have recognized them differently, as initiations, passages through which people deepen their understanding of themselves and the world.

This is where the metaphor of the Human Experience Labyrinth becomes useful.

A Labyrinth contains a single winding path. It moves inward and outward, sometimes bringing the traveler close to the center before spiraling away again. Human life often unfolds in similar ways. People move through cycles of clarity and confusion, grief and renewal, contraction and expansion. These cycles are not signs that something has gone wrong. They are part of the rhythm of growth. To walk the Labyrinth is not to eliminate difficulty. It is to allow the experience to shape us.

> "To live is to suffer, to survive is to find meaning in the suffering. If there is a purpose in life at all, there must be a purpose in suffering and in dying. But no man can tell another what this purpose is. Each must find out for himself, and must accept the responsibility that his answer prescribes. If he succeeds he will continue to grow in spite of all indignities." — Gordon Allport[6]

Meaning Centered

Viktor Frankl's work offers one of the most grounded and enduring perspectives on the role of meaning in human suffering, and his ideas serve as a quiet thread woven throughout this book. As a psychiatrist and Holocaust survivor, Frankl witnessed conditions that stripped individuals of nearly everything—

freedom, dignity, certainty—yet he observed that something essential remained. Even in those circumstances, individuals retained the capacity to choose their relationship to what they were experiencing. From this, he developed Logotherapy, a therapeutic approach centered on the idea that the primary human drive is not pleasure or power, but meaning.[7]

This orientation does not attempt to remove suffering from the human experience, nor does it diminish its weight. Instead, it shifts the question. When suffering cannot be avoided, the focus becomes how it is met, how it is understood, and how it is integrated into the larger arc of a life. Meaning is not something externally assigned or intellectually constructed; it is something discovered through participation in life itself, through what we create, how we love, and how we move through predictable, yet challenging human experiences.

This perspective underlies the Human Experience Labyrinth. While each individual's path is shaped by their own circumstances, there is also a shared structure to the human experience—one that includes moments of expansion and contraction, clarity and confusion, connection and separation. Meaning emerges not from avoiding these movements, but from engaging with them.

As Frankl reminds us, meaning exists, even in the presence of challenge: "Life's meaning is an unconditional one, for it even includes the potential meaning of unavoidable suffering."[8]

The Labyrinth

The Human Experience Labyrinth provides a way of understanding this movement more fully. It is not a model to be mastered, but a framework that helps orient us within the complexity of being human.

The Labyrinth is comprised of concentric circles that represent different layers of experience. The outer layers are often where we first find ourselves immersed in life conditions, duality, disruption, fear, and the immediate realities of being human. These are the catalysts for growth and movement in the Labyrinth. As we move

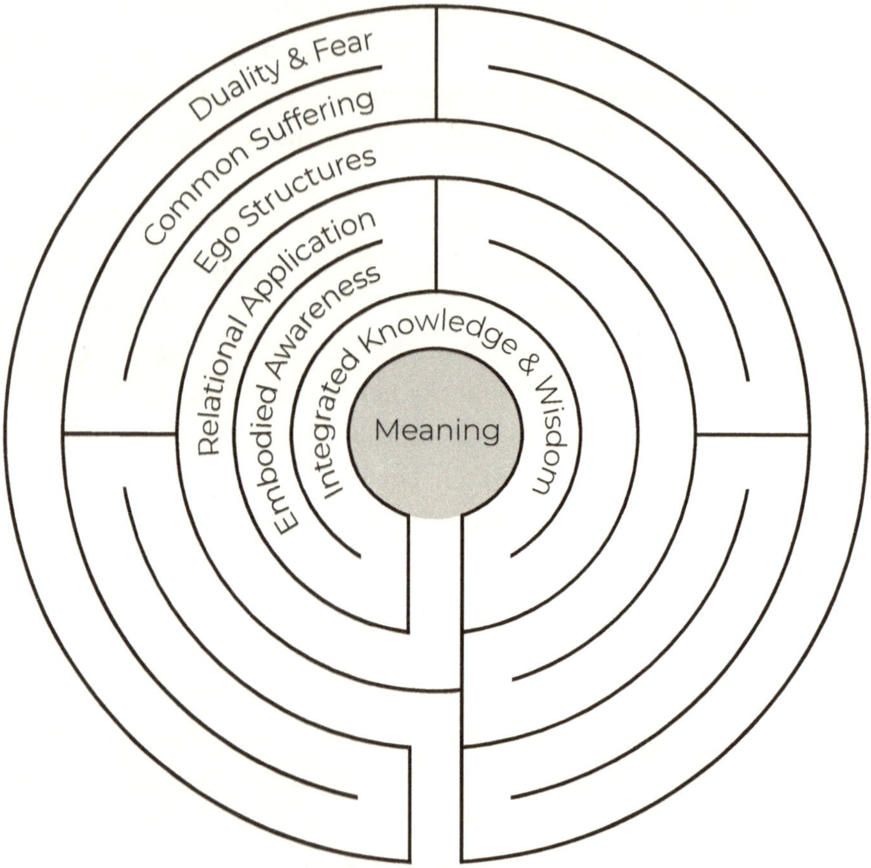

Layer 1	Duality & Fear
Layer 2	Common Suffering
Layer 3	Ego Structures
Layer 4	Relational Application
Layer 5	Embodied Awareness
Layer 6	Integrated Knowledge & Wisdom
Layer 7	Non-Duality and Meaning

inward, we encounter deeper layers of awareness, healing, and integration, until we arrive at the center where meaning, freedom, and non-duality can be experienced.

And yet, the center is not the destination in the way we might expect. It is not a place to remain, nor a state to permanently achieve. The human experience is not about escaping the outer layers, but about moving in relationship with them—into, out of, and around the center, again and again. This movement is the rhythm of life itself.

What holds this entire process is something even more expansive—love. Not as a fleeting emotion, but as the underlying energy that weaves through every part of the experience. It exists within both the most painful and the most joyful aspects of life, allowing for the full spectrum of human experience to be held at once. Love is not about living in and experiencing only the light. Love is the energy that holds the entirety of life—the things we perceive as good and bad. It is the feeling of excruciating beauty and the peace that comes from accepting and seeing it all as part of the big beautiful, and intentional play. It is the very thin coin that holds joy on one side and grief on the other.

The Human Experience Labyrinth is comprised of seven layers.

Layer	Elements
Outer Layers (Surface Experience)	Life Conditions; Duality; Suffering; Disruption; Fear
Inner Layers (Process)	Disintegration, Remembering; Healing; Awareness; Integration
Center (Core State)	Meaning; Freedom; Non-duality

Layers 1 & 2: Duality and the Beginning of the Path

At the outermost layer of the Labyrinth, we encounter duality. This is the realm of separation—the experience of self and other, light and dark, pleasure and pain. It is where we are most fully immersed in our human story and our physical form. While duality

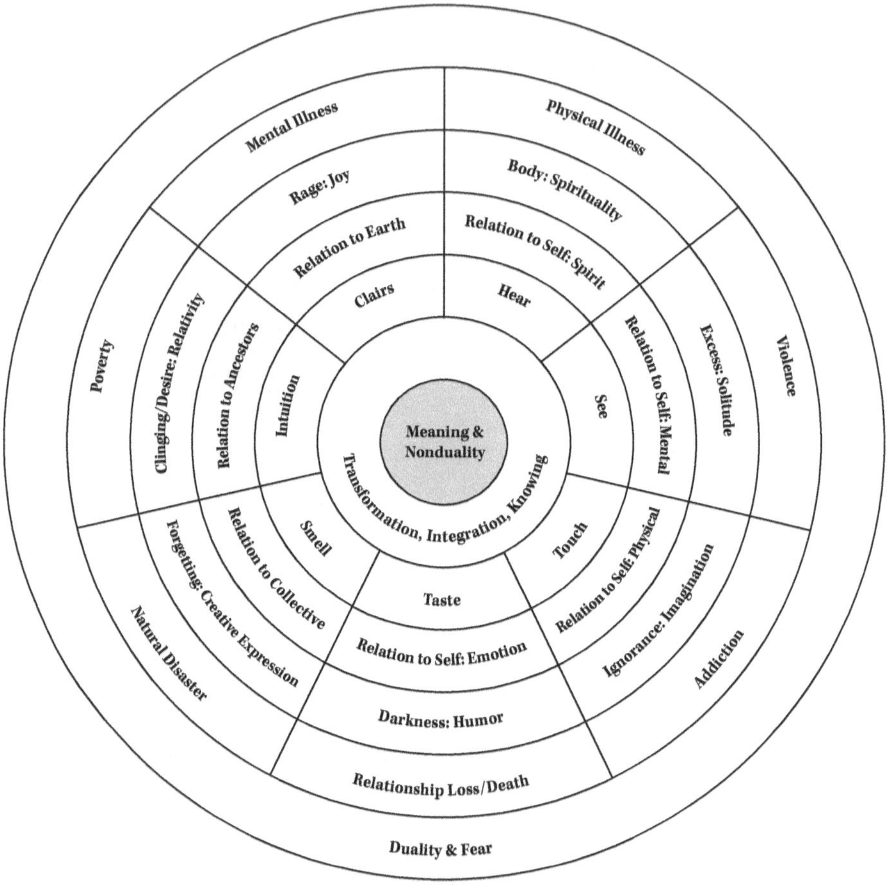

is often seen as something to transcend, it is also the very mechanism through which we come to know anything at all. We cannot understand light without darkness, nor joy without sorrow. While duality serves its purpose, when seen from a place of fear instead of understanding, it can create a negative and limiting approach to life. When we can only see things as separate we often operate from a place of fear—we may think in terms of me versus them, I'm alone and need to figure everything out myself, my individual survival is dependent on me. In life, we can generally choose to act from either love or fear. Love knows no separation, has faith and trust, and feels supported. Fear thrives on separation and prevents us from letting our guards down and truly connecting with the many relationships we have in life (to the various parts of self, to others, and to the earth). We can either enter into challenging life experiences from a place of love or fear—and this orientation significantly changes how we move through the Labyrinth. Fear is not a layer to be mastered, but one that weaves it's way through the entire Labyrinth. We are continually challenged to move past fear—fear of fully feeling, fear of truly being seen and connecting, fear of disintegration, surrender and acceptance, etc.

As we move through life, we inevitably encounter experiences that disrupt our sense of stability—loss, illness, violence, disconnection, or change. These are not anomalies; they are common and predictable parts of the human experience. These moments often act as catalysts, breaking open previously held assumptions and creating opportunities for deeper understanding.

The common experiences that open our hearts and break us down are the opportunities to know ourselves better, and what can often lead to Post-Traumatic Growth.[9] In our lifetimes, each and every one of us will experience at least one of these:

- Natural Disaster
- Poverty
- Mental Health Condition
- Physical Health Condition
- Violence
- Addiction
- Relationship Loss/Death

As a product of going through a challenging experience, our ego begins to do its work. Ego is the survival instinct—the stories we build to survive our traumas and fears. It's the labels, performance, and structures we build as protective armor that requires us to see ourselves as separate.

Layer 3: The Role of the Ego

In response to these disruptions, the ego begins to form its structures. The ego is not something to be eliminated; it is a survival mechanism. It organizes experience, creates narratives, and helps us navigate the world. It is the part of us that builds identity, adapts to circumstances, and attempts to maintain a sense of control and safety.

However, the ego can also become rigid. It can cling, defend, compare, and distort in ways that limit our ability to fully experience life. Traditionally, these tendencies have been framed as flaws or moral failings, often described through constructs like the "seven deadly sins." But what if these aspects of the ego are not problems to eradicate, but invitations to deeper awareness?

These tendencies can be reframed as universal powers—darkness, desire, ignorance, excess, forgetfulness, embodiment, and rage. When approached with curiosity rather than judgment, each of these experiences offers a pathway to its opposite: humor, perspective, imagination, solitude, creative expression, spirituality, and joy.

We are not trying to kill the ego. We are simply using it to fully know ourselves. Can we be grateful for and embrace the role of the ego? Embracing the ego doesn't mean that we let it run rampant. We do need to counter its negative tendency—and we do that with their opposite. These challenges spark and illuminate the following opposing experiences and expressions:

1. Darkness: Humor
2. Clinging/Desire: Relativity & Zooming Out
3. Ignorance: Imagination/Internal World Exploration
4. Excess: Solitude
5. Forgetting: Creative Expression
6. The Body: Spirituality/Prayer
7. Rage: Joy

Our current paradigm of the human experience stops here at the ego level. We see ourselves as separate, experience immense pain and suffering, and respond to it with our ego. The systems in place reinforce individuality, a need to change whatever caused the challenge, and therapy to manage the parts of the ego that want to be destructive or cause pain.

In recent years though, there has been a shift toward incorporating the mind, body, and soul as a means of nervous system regulation. I believe this is the start of our attunement to and awareness of the next layer, which is our relationship to all of the parts that make up our whole. We literally cannot access the deeper layers if our nervous system is not resourced and mostly regulated.

In this way, the ego becomes a teacher. It reveals where we are holding tightly, where we are disconnected, and where growth is possible. The work is not to suppress these experiences, but to move through them—to allow them to expand our awareness rather than constrain it.

Layer 4: Relationship and Interconnection

As awareness deepens, the focus begins to shift outward again—not in separation, but in relationship. The fourth layer of the Labyrinth reflects our connection to the many parts that make up our existence: our emotional and physical selves, our thoughts, our relationships, our ancestors, the collective, and the natural world.

This layer is grounded in principles drawn from Indigenous teachings—respect, responsibility, reciprocity, and right relationship. These principles remind us that we do not exist in isolation. Our well-being is interconnected with the well-being of others, the land, and the systems we are part of. To live in right relationship is to move with awareness of this interconnectedness, to recognize both what we receive and what we give, and to take responsibility for the ways we participate in the world.

Layer 5: Expanding Awareness

From this place of connection, our perception begins to expand. While we often rely on the five physical senses to understand reality, they offer only a limited view. As we deepen our relationship with ourselves and our environment, other forms of knowing begin to emerge—intuition, insight, and forms of perception that are less tangible but equally real.

These capacities, sometimes referred to as the "clairs," include clear seeing, hearing, feeling, and knowing. These are often sensed internally rather than experienced as physical manifestations. They are not separate from the human experience, but extensions of it, becoming more accessible as we cultivate presence, awareness, and full embodiment. This is where full mind-body connection and integration lives.

Layer 6: Integration and Transformation

As these layers begin to come together, we enter a phase of integration. Knowledge becomes embodied. Insight becomes lived experience. There is a willingness to feel more fully, to allow for both expansion and contraction, and to move with greater trust in the process. When we are able to listen to and sense what the body is telling us, we learn to trust ourselves and know through feeling when we are out of right relationship. When I have been too busy and too stressed to listen to my body, I second-guess myself and accept other's opinions of me as truth. When I am able to listen to my body, I realize that I can trust myself. I know the feeling it gives me when something is out of alignment, and I can then check in to make a change. I no longer rely on outside feedback as my barometer of personal truth.

At the center of the Labyrinth, there are moments where meaning becomes clear, where the separation between self and experience softens, and where a sense of alignment emerges. But these moments are not meant to be held onto. They are part of the larger rhythm of returning—again and again—to the path. This is not a state of permanent peace or resolution. Rather, it is a deepening capacity to engage with life as it unfolds. Moments of clarity arise, followed by moments of forgetting. Periods of connection are followed by disconnection. The movement continues.

Layer 7: Freedom

Freedom is often initially seen as the ability to do whatever you want. The definition for many evolves to being able to choose—

even if the choice is one of commitment and dedication—that may limit one's ability to do anything and everything. Eventually, the definition refines itself to the peace that surpasses all understanding. Once one can clearly see and feel how the entire human experience has led to this moment—to alignment and to clarity—a sense of freedom from the impact of external conditions becomes available. Freedom is acceptance of the fullness of the human experience and gratitude for all it brings. When we can surrender to and allow for what is, we stop gripping and begin flowing. Freedom is not finding happiness, but working through and shedding the layers of fear and ego that have kept you from yourself. It's finding the meaning of your unique existence. You can't find freedom, peace, or meaning by chasing it—that's like a dog chasing its own tail. You are already it.

Full Presence

> "Your hand opens and closes, opens and closes. If it were always a fist or always stretched open, you would be paralyzed. Your deepest presence is in every small contracting and expanding, the two as beautifully balanced and coordinated as birds' wings." —Jalal al-Din Rumi, "Birdwings"

When we make the goal a permanently open hand (e.g., elation, ecstasy, happiness, comfort), we are setting ourselves up for failure. It is flowing with and being fully immersed in the dance of opening and closing that is the goal. We can't know one without the other. We need duality and contrast to fully know ourselves. When we flow with and fully feel the immense range of experience that lies between duality and non-duality, instead of resisting, we eliminate suffering. We will still feel the full range of emotions, which includes those we label as hard or bad, but suffering comes from resistance to, holding onto, and/or identification with a feeling.

When society makes happiness the goal, we believe that if we aren't happy, there is something wrong with us that needs to be fixed. And then we turn to medication or substances—prescribed or not—to do the work for us, when in reality, instead of helping us to be happy, it strips us of the opportunity to be in our full human experience. When we prioritize happiness, we give up reaping the rewards that come on the other side of the unraveling and messiness. When happiness and comfort are the goal, we are set up for failure. As Rumi's poem so eloquently states, if we were paralyzed in a permanent state of happiness, we would never get to know our fullest presence.[10] The universal human experience is that of birth *and* death, creation *and* destruction, compassion *and* violence. When we live in the reality of duality, happiness as the goal is not only a losing proposition, but one that keeps us stuck and eventually hopeless.

While there are many formal interventions that may be effective but require formal training, one thing we can all offer is full presence. How often have you experienced someone fully with you—listening, feeling, attuning to, and be-ing with you? How often are you truly present with yourself? We often go through life on autopilot—not stopping to truly listen and connect—both with ourselves and others. True presence requires time, space, stillness, and attention. It allows for us to be with what is in the moment instead of numbing or focusing on the past or future. It is a rare, but potent experience. Presence is free, limitless, and is one of the most powerful connectors and regulators there is. The concept of co-regulation speaks to the power of presence. When someone is present and attuned to you, they are literally able to create an environment for your nervous system to be resourced and to regulate. Just by holding space, in presence.

Creating Capacity

In a recent therapeutic plant medicine journey, I saw the entirety of what I had been through in my life. It was overwhelming as I saw the amount of pain that I had not processed. As I was resisting feeling it all, I told my guide that I didn't want to have a pity party for myself. This is how I had lived my life ... trying to be strong and not feel sorry for myself. But in the process of that, I resisted very real emotions. Those emotions don't go away—they just hide and accumulate. My guide told me that having a "pity party" (aka allowing myself to take the time and space to feel the depth of my experiences) is exactly what I needed to do. I needed to feel it all and process it. The plant medicine was the conduit for stepping through the fear of feeling and providing capacity for my nervous system to meet big emotions. It provided enough of a buffer for me to actually face what I had been through and acknowledge its impact on me. I felt the contractions and literal physical pain in my stomach, heart, and throat. And on the other side of that somatic and emotional processing, there was so much spaciousness and lightness. I was tender for sure, but the density and weight of all of those unfelt emotions moved through my body.

Much of this book is dedicated to the discussion of practical applications for how to create capacity. We aren't resisting feeling just because it's uncomfortable. As a society, we have not created environments or containers that can hold the mess that comes with fully feeling. In order to fully feel, we must first know that those around us can handle it. That they are willing to be present and witness it. As individuals, we must also know that we have resources to pull on to ensure that we can handle it.

How do we reimagine our work as human beings, from being happy and comfortable, to fully feeling and experiencing all emotions (pain included) without suffering? This isn't possible without creating capacity within ourselves, communities, and social structures to witness, hold, and feel it all—to be with what is. What if instead of trying to change, hide, or bury our realities to make it feel better, we could create capacity within ourselves to be in all of it?

CHAPTER 2:

Walking the Human Experience Labyrinth

"Life's meaning is an unconditional one, for it even includes the potential meaning of unavoidable suffering."
—Viktor Frankl, *Man's Search For Meaning*

To walk the Labyrinth is not to solve a problem, but to enter into a relationship with the full spectrum of your life. It is an opportunity to see life's experiences as "grist for the mill" as Ram Dass would say.[11] When Noah passed, I felt a strong determination to not let my grief "go to waste." It has been the largest piece of grist for the mill that I have experienced. I want to squeeze every last bit of learning and growth I can get from it. I want to make it meaningful. The meaning and learning have had to match the depth of pain and love that I feel. And that is enormous.

We are conditioned to approach challenges as something to figure out, fix, or move beyond as quickly as possible. We look for the most efficient path, the clearest answer, the fastest relief. But the Labyrinth offers a different invitation. It asks us to slow down, to remain present, and to trust that meaning is not found by escaping the path, but by walking it.

At times, the path will feel steady and clear. At others, it will feel disorienting, as though you are moving away from where you think you should be. There will be moments of closeness to the center—of insight, peace, or clarity—followed by moments that pull you outward again into uncertainty, discomfort, or confusion. This is not a mistake. It is the nature of the path.

Walking the Labyrinth requires a willingness to let go of the need to control the experience and instead cultivate the capacity to be with it. It asks for presence over perfection, curiosity over certainty, and engagement over avoidance. Each turn offers something, not always what we want, but often what we need in order to deepen our understanding of ourselves and our place in the world.

This is not a passive process. It is an active, lived practice. It is intentional. It is the way we meet our grief, our joy, our fear, our connection, and our meaning. It is how we return to ourselves, again and again, not as fixed or finished beings, but as people continually unfolding.

As you move forward, the Labyrinth becomes less of something you walk and more of something you live. Each experience, each relationship, each moment of contraction and expansion becomes part of the path. You begin to recognize that there is no final arrival, only deeper layers of awareness and integration.

The invitation is not to reach the center and stay there, but to walk with greater understanding, to return with greater wisdom, and to carry what you discover into the way you live, relate, and contribute to the world.

This is the practice of walking the Labyrinth.

In Section I of this book, we have briefly covered each component listed in each of the seven layers of the Labyrinth and how they relate to each other and work together to form a comprehensive picture of how and why humans move through each layer.

Section II of this book provides a critical analysis of how our current reality of only acknowledging, being aware of, and creating systems to address the outermost Layers (1, 2 and 3) is a very limited and stunted approach to the human experience that will continue to result in suffering and/or dissociation. This current approach to mental health is a mix of psychotherapy, ego and nervous system regulation skills, psychoeducation, and medication.

With the whole experience in mind, in Section III of this book, we then reimagine how we recognize and interact with the outermost layers while shedding light on how we can acknowledge and work with the innermost layers through more somatic practices, Soul Work,[12] and transpersonal approaches (Layers 4, 5, 6, and 7). There is a heavy emphasis on the relational Layer (4) as this is where much of our day to day existence lies.

The Seven Layers & Associated Approaches to Walking the Path

The figure below depicts where each approach to address and support human growth lives within the Labyrinth.

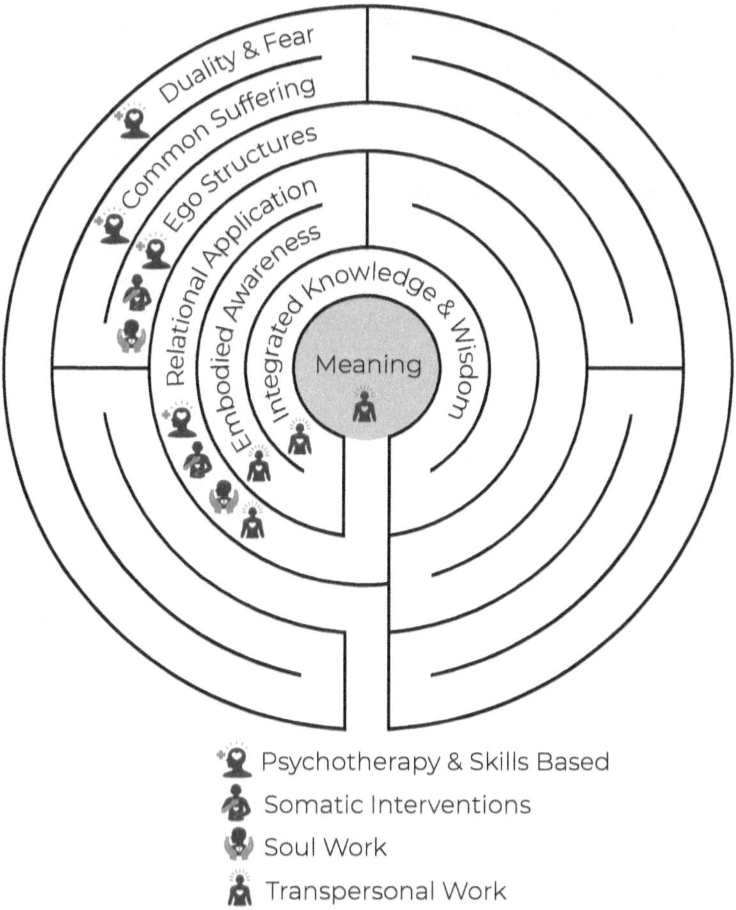

Human Experience Labyrinth Layer	Interventions or Approaches for Growth and Movement within that Layer
Layer 1: Duality & Fear	Psychotherapy/Psychoeducation
Layer 2: Common Suffering	Psychotherapy/Psychoeducation
Layer 3: Ego Structures	Psychotherapy/Psychoeducation
Layer 4: Relational Application	Somatic, Soul Work, Transpersonal
Layer 5: Embodied Awareness	Somatic, Soul Work, Transpersonal
Layer 6: Integrated Knowledge & Wisdom	Soul Work, Transpersonal
Layer 7: Non-Duality and Meaning	Transpersonal

Moving beyond the discussion of psychotherapy and psychoeducation found in the outer layers of the Labyrinth, somatic work focuses on the connection between the mind and body, helping individuals process and regulate their experiences through physical awareness and sensation.

Soul Work builds on this by integrating both spiritual insight and practical application, supporting a deeper sense of peace and alignment in daily life. Soul Work seeks to understand and integrate the following concepts:

- Suffering
- Connecting With our Innate Wisdom
- Control
- Fear
- Post Traumatic Growth
- Listening, Leaning In, and Softening
- Stillness
- Presence
- Non-attachment
- Perspective
- Acceptance
- Consciousness Studies
- Lessons from Nature
- Processing and Integration

Transpersonal approaches expand this integration further, incorporating spiritual, transcendent, and consciousness-based experiences into modern psychology. Together, these perspectives move beyond an ego-centered understanding of the self, exploring human potential, peak experiences, and a sense of unity, with the aim of supporting the whole person and their relationship and connection within themselves, and to that which is sensed as external to them.

Application of Maslow's Hierarchy of Needs

Just as Maslow's Hierarchy of Need suggests, we have foundations that need to be built in order to move through the human experience. Maslow's hierarchy has been criticized due to its rigid nature of hierarchy. This is where the Labyrinth framework can prove helpful. Humans are not stuck on one layer—they likely have a foot in many layers at once, but with more time and energy devoted to one than the rest. We can use some nervous system regulation tools, while also utilizing community support, while also working on trusting oneself, while also connecting to spirit. The key is to not get stuck or solely rely on one "level," which often happens in Western approaches to treatment.

The Human Experience Labyrinth expands Maslow's hierarchy by providing more nuance and clarity around the wholeness of the process toward self-actualization and meaning-making.

Human Experience Labyrinth	Maslow's Hierarchy of Needs
Physical Safety / Duality (Layers 1 & 2)	Physiological Needs
Ego/Nervous System Regulation (Layer 3)	Safety Needs
Relationships (Layer 4)	Love & Belonging
Full Senses, Knowing & Transformation (Layers 5 & 6)	Esteem Needs
Meaning (Layer 7)	Self-Actualization

Maslow's hierarchy has also been criticized because it emphasizes the individualistic culture's focus on self-actualization over collective culture's focus on community wellbeing or a meaning-centered goal, which generally is inspired by how one can give back or be of service. Once again, we find ourselves in a black and white narrative. It seems that perhaps each culture's orientation, situated at opposite poles, could benefit from meeting somewhere in the middle. As many collective nations find themselves being introduced to increased industrialization and technologies that give them more time in the day (as this time no longer needs to be used to maintain physiological safety) they can allow more time to devote to esteem and self actualization work. And at the other end of the pole, fully industrialized nations that allow time and space for internal contemplation can benefit from returning to tending to their bodies, the land, and each other. There are other cultures we can turn to for inspiration, such as -Indigenous South America, that are both collectivist and have a strong emphasis on the development of individual awareness through the use of group experiences with plant medicines.

Again, as with everything, I propose seeing things from an *and* perspective instead of *or*. We must meet somewhere in the middle. Yes, we need coping skills, *and* we need to fully feel the impact of an experience. Yes, we need to address distress and suffering, *and* we need to allow for the full expression of emotion. Yes, we need to process trauma physiologically in the brain, *and* we need to go deeper to integrate the pieces of trauma that are spiritual (e.g. shame, acceptance, forgiveness (for self and others), etc.) Yes, we need to work on our individual well-being, *and* we need to consider the collective.

SECTION II:

A Critique of the Current System

Pathologizing the Human Experience

"It is sacred to feel. I do not owe the world a mask when sorrow rises like mist from the soul. To fall apart is not weakness, it is a rite of release, a passage the ancestors once walked with grace. Let me be true, even in my unraveling." —DailyShaman on Facebook[13]

Individual vs. Communal

The idea that we even have a "system" for mental health is an alarming red flag that we have a problem. How have we gotten so far away from our relationship and connection to nature, to ourselves, to community, and to something greater that we rely on strangers who we can see for fifty minutes at a time, who are getting paid to see us, and who are often trained or required by insurance to help us get to a point of "functional" as soon as possible? The real impact on our well-being does not come from transactional relationships that have limits, guidelines, and were formulated to fit our capitalist society, where getting back to a state of productivity as soon as possible is the goal. True healing and awakening should be accessible to everyone—and it is—if we can remember that the goal is to walk the path to know ourselves, instead of getting as close to twenty-four-hour happiness and comfort as possible. We don't always need fancy interventions delivered only by those who have been formally trained or received a certification. Often, we need simple presence, to be held, witnessed, and attuned to. We need wisdom, models, elders, time, space, and community. We need existing social structures to have the ability to be with and hold the entirety of the human experience. Other cultures that have not been as impacted by industrialization, capitalism, and the medical model can offer us inspiration and guidance.

The way we view grief and death is a prime example. Many cultures integrate grief into their way of being. In the Jewish tradition, sitting shiva for a week after a death is standard. In Latin America, our ancestors are honored with the celebration of Dia de los Muertos. In modern Western psychology, grief is often approached as an individual, internal medical process, whereas communal traditions view it as a collective, external social responsibility. This shift from communal to individualistic models has significant implications for how people experience "closure" and healing. In our haste to get people to feel better as quickly as possible, we inadvertently create pressure and stifled processes which lead to states for which we have created pathologized diagnosis, like "prolonged grief" and "complicated grief." This may be the definition of insanity. We are literally creating the environments which lead to the pathologies that we make up to make sense of why people are struggling. We are so far in it that we can't see we are the creators of our own problems.

Individualistic vs. Communal Models of Grief

Feature	Modern Western (Individualistic)	Traditional (Communal)
Primary Goal	Resolution: Moving through "stages" to return to "normal."	Integration: Carrying the deceased forward with the community.
Location	Private: Therapy offices, bedrooms, or clinical settings.	Public: The home, the village square.
Role of Others	Passive: "Let me know if you need anything."	Active: Taking over the mourner's chores, meals, and social duties.
Timeline	Linear: Expectation to "get back to work" quickly.	Cyclical: Recurring rituals (anniversaries, bone-turning).
Expression	Controlled: Dignified silence or private weeping.	Cathartic: Public wailing, dancing, or loud storytelling.

The most famous framework on grief that is focused on the individual experience is the Elizabeth Kübler-Ross model of stages of grief (Denial, Anger, Bargaining, Depression, Acceptance).[14] While helpful for identifying the expression of emotions, in recent years critics have argued that it can inadvertently pressure individuals to "perform" grief correctly or "finish" it by moving through each of the stages. In the clinical focus, grief is often pathologized. If a person grieves "too long," they may be diagnosed with "Prolonged Grief Disorder." Most work places offer three days of leave after a loved one has passed. In a communal setting, you don't have to decide how to grieve; the culture provides the script. In an individualistic setting, the mourner must often invent their own rituals, which can be exhausting during a time of low energy.

In many Indigenous and traditional cultures, grief is not something you "get over," but something you renegotiate. "Double Burden" refers to having to deal with life while at the same time dealing with grief. Relief is found in communal models: The community recognizes that the mourner is temporarily "out of commission." By bringing food (like the Seudat Havara'ah in Judaism) or managing the estate, the community removes the "work of living" so the mourner can do the "work of grieving." Communal rituals create a physical container. When people "Sit Shiva," the constant presence of a minyan ensures that the silence of the house is filled with human warmth. It prevents the "grief hole"—the feeling of being swallowed by an empty house.

Communal grief is an act of reciprocity and responsibility. Reciprocity is demonstrated by the community supporting the mourner today, knowing that the mourner will support others in the future. Responsibility is demonstrated as the "right action" of the tribe to ensure that the spirit of the deceased is honored and that the living are not lost to despair. There is a growing movement in Western psychology called Continuing Bonds Theory.[15] It moves away from "letting go" and toward the communal idea of maintaining a relationship with the deceased through memory, ritual, and "right action" in their name.

Modern Western movements are increasingly challenging the "death taboo" by creating intentional community spaces that prioritize shared human experience over individual, clinical resolution. These initiatives aim to build grief literacy—the skills and values needed to respond compassionately to loss by shifting death and dying back into communal spaces. Examples of this include Death Cafés, where strangers meet to discuss mortality over tea and cake, with no set agenda or intention to lead participants to a specific conclusion and grief circles where, unlike traditional therapy groups, are often rooted in "grief tending"—a practice that incorporates ritual, storytelling, and creativity. Participants are invited to share their grief while others act as "witnesses." Listeners do not offer advice or "cross-talk" but acknowledge the sharer with simple phrases like "I see you." These circles are non-hierarchical; the facilitator is a participant who also shares their own humanity. There has also been a recent Death Positive Movement with organizations and the role of death doulas[16] created to advocate for a radical shift in how Westerners engage with mortality.

Death is the one thing that we know for certain will happen to all of us. Distress from the other common sufferings have similar societal reactions. Often, people will respond to distressing events such as divorce, illness, job loss, substance abuse, etc., with some form of resistance to its presence through a stress response—depression, anxiety, anger, overwhelm, etc. When this happens, we offer the response of a diagnosis and turn to what research says about which formalized interventions and resources are best for that specific diagnosis.

Alcoholics Anonymous and other free support groups are great examples of services that appear to have found a hybrid structure based in community, offering shared wisdom and experience, and are accessible and not transactional. These support groups are formalized enough to be accessible to anyone in our individualistic society who may not already have integrated and organic support in their families or communities.

It is clear that even as Western culture attempts to return to communal holding roots, because our communities are not currently set up to do this work, if we do not have a religious affiliation or church, often we lean on formal structures (paid death doulas, paid grief circles, paid therapists, etc.). Relying on formal supports that require payment or are only offered when a specific leader decides to offer it creates a structure in which some can access services and some can't. There are barriers. Care often turns into a transactional offering. Perhaps the greatest limitation of the current system is not its lack of resources, but its underlying assumption that human suffering can be adequately addressed through transactional interventions alone.

CHAPTER 3:

Diagnosis and Pharmaceuticals

DSM

As caring and empathetic people who don't like to see others in pain, we want to be as effective and efficient as possible to return someone to their most productive and comfortable state. But that's not what the human experience is. It's a messy, never-ending spiral of challenge and growth. When we put expectations on people that they should be better after starting medication or going to therapy, then it creates a dangerous emotional backlash when they ultimately don't feel better and have "failed" at helping themselves. Did you know that the suicide risk increases significantly following a mental health diagnosis, with the highest risk occurring shortly after initial diagnosis or psychiatric discharge? Studies indicate that up to 51 percent of individuals who die by suicide had a diagnosed mental health condition in the year prior. The risk is particularly elevated for bipolar disorder, schizophrenia, and depression, with rates often five to thirteen times higher than the general population.[17] Environments become ripe with hopelessness, despair and suicidality when someone feels like they are destined to suffer because they haven't been helped by the only resources they know to be available and what society tells them should work.

Did you know that the *Diagnostic Statistics Manual* (DSM) is a guide used by therapists to label, diagnose, and treat, and it was created for insurance companies to bill for services? This is a prime example of how our realities are socially constructed. We decided to pathologize the human experience because of a billing and efficiency need.[18] Imagine if that had never happened ... would our mental health crisis exist the same way it does now? Sure, we would still have people who are suffering, but it wouldn't be pathologized, and a fast and effective way for the person to feel better (so insurance companies don't have to pay too much for too long and big pharma makes lots of money) wouldn't be the standard. Instead, the lows of the human experience would just be considered part of the human experience, and they would be given the time and space needed to be tended to, integrated, and passed through.

Students training to become therapists often enter a system that, without intending harm, positions them as participants in a larger, socially constructed framework—one that prioritizes diagnosis and efficiency as foundational elements of care. Much of their education centers on the Diagnostic and Statistical Manual (DSM), shaping how they learn to understand and respond to human distress. This framework is closely tied to insurance reimbursement models, which frequently limit the number of sessions available and incentivize brief, outcome-oriented approaches. Interventions such as Solution-Focused Therapy have emerged in part as a response to these constraints, offering practical, effective tools for helping individuals identify goals, access strengths, and create movement in relatively short periods of time.[19] In many cases—particularly in acute or situational distress—this approach can be incredibly valuable.

At the same time, when brief, solution-oriented models become the default rather than one tool among many, they can unintentionally narrow the scope of care. Not all human experiences lend themselves to quick resolution. Grief, identity shifts, trauma, and existential questioning often require space, time, and deeper exploration that extends beyond identifying a "solution." The concern is not with Solution-Focused Therapy itself, but with a system that may over-rely on it due to structural pressures, potentially leaving both clients and clinicians without the capacity to engage in the fuller, more complex work of meaning-making and integration. Studies on the effectiveness of current mental health interventions are often asking questions based on symptom reduction, not growth or meaning making. So, while research may indicate effectiveness, we have to ask ourselves, effective at what? The process of soul learning and evolution needs time, space—and more than talk therapy and medications that can dull the full expression of the experience. How have we lost sight of the need to feel and experience life as it is instead of muffling or silencing it?

Some might say, "Sure, I can get on board with that if we're talking about minor depression or anxiety, but what about the really problematic mental health diagnoses like schizophrenia, bipolar, or full blown psychosis?" When we can look to other cultures and see how they approach the same symptoms differently, it becomes clear that our diagnosis and subsequent treatment might be influenced by our social construction of reality and may not be the absolute truth. This is exemplified in the Native American culture where often, Schizophrenia is seen as someone who has all of their senses on board—including their "clairs." In Western culture, they are seen as "crazy" because they are experiencing more than the limited reality that most of us experience. They often don't know why they are different and they experience additional suffering because they are pathologized and made to feel crazy. They may also be experiencing a deep disconnection between the inner reality they know to be true and the trauma and/or dysfunctional society in which they are living. This inability to understand what is "true" or "real" is the definition of psychosis. What if their internal experiences and feelings were validated and there was acknowledgment of the sick and dysfunctional systems in which we live?

There is a growing acknowledgment that, many times, a spiritual awakening is seen as psychosis. When going through a spiritual awakening, one feels like they are outside of "normal" reality; they are disoriented and may have impaired functioning. If this is seen as psychosis, the person may be medicated or hospitalized. If the person is met with normalization and understanding, it has the potential to lead to growth, clarity, and integration into "normal" life.[20]

It is important to consider the lens through which we see mental health and diagnosis. Other cultures view the same symptoms or characteristics that we pathologize, differently. Schizophrenia occurs in Native American populations at rates similar to the general U.S. population, but cultural differences significantly shape symptom expression and interpretation (e.g., spiritual vs. medical). Native American interpretations of bipolar disorder often frame symptoms not just as individual pathology, but as manifestations of historical trauma, systemic disenfranchisement, and disconnection from community or nature. Some traditional perspectives also interpret symptoms like mania or depression as a disruption in the person's connection to their surroundings or a manifestation of external, energetic forces. These views emphasize a holistic, spiritual, and communal approach to healing, using traditional and land-based practices to restore balance rather than relying solely on Western medical models.[21]

Key perspectives and approaches include:

- Contextualizing Trauma: Rather than simply labeling behaviors as "crazy," many Indigenous perspectives interpret mental health struggles as responses to intense, generational, or systemic adversity.
- Holistic Healing: Recovery is often viewed as finding a "restored balance" through holistic approaches that address spiritual, mental, and communal needs, rather than just physical
- Cultural Connection: Strengthening ties to culture, tradition, and elders is considered vital for mental health.
- Need for Culturally Appropriate Care: There is a call for mental healthcare that aligns with Indigenous worldviews and healing paradigms, potentially reducing reliance on medication alone.

Understanding various approaches to the same symptoms across various cultures allows us to zoom out and question whether our approach is the "right" one. The Western approach seems to be one often based on fear and control. It is quite scary to see someone who is struggling to be in the dysfunctional social reality we've created when that reality does not readily acknowledge, foster, and support our connection to ourselves, to each other, to nature, and to something greater. The person who sees clearly or feels deeply how dysfunctional our current system is can be made to feel crazy when the dysfunction is not acknowledged by society or the systems that we interact with each day.

The image below is a light hearted depiction of how this can feel. While everyone is swimming in a contaminated pool (dysfunctional society), they see the person who is not, as the problem. This can feel isolating, disorienting, and maddening.

Image generated by ChatGPT, March 15, 2026, from the prompt, "Create an image showing a person in the middle of a pool surrounded by people pointing at them. The pool is yellow on the outside and clear surrounding the person in the middle."

"An abnormal reaction to an abnormal situation is normal behaviour." —Viktor Frankl, *Man's Search for Meaning*

I am not pretending to know what the "right" answer is in response to each and every mental health challenge. We lean into the concept of *and* again. There are certainly people whose mental health challenges stabilize with medication and evidence based therapies, which then allows them to do the deep work that is required of this life. *And*, I do encourage a deeper and more nuanced examination of our current approach and a consideration of a more holistic view. I am advocating to include an expanded view and consideration of the human experience when considering how we approach mental and emotional health, and I am encouraging more stringent diagnosis screenings so that medication is used only when truly necessary.

Big Pharma, Antidepressants, and Suicidality

If antidepressants are a big part of the answer, why have depression, anxiety, and suicide rates increased exponentially over the past twenty years despite the increased use of antidepressants? There is a clear correlation among the increase in mental health challenges, the increase in the use of technology and decreased opportunity for real-life connection, and the increase in using antidepressants to manage fallout from this feeling of disconnection. The problem is that we're attempting to manage this lack of connection with something that mutes our ability to truly feel and connect. We are unaware of how our treatment is exacerbating the issue.

- In 2023, approximately 11.4 percent of U.S. adults reported taking prescription medication for depression, with higher usage among women (15.3 percent) compared to men (7.4 percent). Antidepressant use generally increases with age, particularly for those forty and older, with 19.1 percent of adults over sixty taking them. Usage has risen significantly, with a 66 percent increase in dispensing rates for young adults between 2016 and 2022.[22]

- The prevalence of depression in adolescents and adults age twelve and older increased from 8.2 percent to 13.1 percent from 2013 to 2023.[23]
- A significant increase was seen in the percentage of adults with anxiety symptoms (from 15.6 to 18.2 percent, respectively) and depression symptoms (from 18.5 to 21.4 percent, respectively) between 2019 and 2022.[24]
- Suicide rates increased 37 percent from 2000 to 2018 and decreased 5 percent from 2018 to 2020. However, rates returned to their peak in 2022.[25]

Big Pharma has spent decades persuading the public that despair is a chemical error, that depression is a defect in serotonin, and that suffering can be corrected through compliance with a prescription. This story—simple, soothing, and profitable—was never solid science. It was marketing.[26]

The now-famous "chemical imbalance" explanation for depression has not held up under scrutiny. Large-scale reviews have found no consistent evidence that depression is caused by low serotonin levels in the brain or a deficit in serotonergic activity.[27] Even major research institutions have acknowledged that the theory was oversimplified and overstated, presented publicly as fact long after the evidence failed to support it.[28] And yet, the drugs justified by that story continue to dominate mental health care.

This matters because it reframes what antidepressants actually are. They are not correcting a proven biological malfunction. They are psychoactive substances that alter brain states—sometimes in ways people experience as relief, and sometimes in ways that produce emotional numbing, agitation, or dissociation. To call that "treatment" without nuance is to obscure risk.

The strongest defenses of Selective Serotonin Reuptake Inhibitors (SSRIs) often point to meta-analyses showing that antidepressants outperform placebos on average in short-term trials.[29] But "statistically significant" is not the same as clinically meaningful. Many meta-analyses demonstrate that the average benefit (effect size) is modest and unevenly distributed, and that the most robust benefits tend to occur in severe cases.[30] A drug can beat a placebo in trials and still fail to meaningfully improve real-world outcomes at scale.

This gap between marketing and lived experience has consequences. Patients report feeling emotionally flattened rather than healed. They describe increased agitation, inner restlessness, and suicidal thoughts early in treatment, only to be told these reactions are symptoms of the illness rather than potential effects of the drug.[31] When distress intensifies after starting medication, the response is rarely curiosity. It is escalation: higher doses, additional diagnoses, more medications.

Nowhere is this more ethically fraught than with children and adolescents. Regulatory agencies have acknowledged that antidepressants are associated with increased risk of suicidal thinking and behavior in youth, particularly early in treatment.[32] Even with "black box" warnings, the risks are often minimized or reframed, with insufficient attention to individual variability in response.

What the system continues to avoid is the deeper reckoning that depression and suicidality are not merely biochemical events. They are often responses—to trauma, isolation, economic precarity, racism, moral injury, violence, and a culture that treats people as commodities.[33] Reducing these realities to neurotransmitters allows institutions to sidestep responsibility for the social conditions that shape emotional suffering.

Psychiatry, under pressure from pharmaceutical influence, has too often become procedural rather than relational. Fifteen-minute visits. Checklists. Symptom suppression instead of meaning-centered care. Presence replaced by protocol. The human soul, treated as collateral damage. And the most dangerous lie persists: If the medication doesn't work, the patient is the problem. This framework leaves no room for grief that makes sense, rage that is justified, or despair that is rational in an unjust world. It collapses moral and social suffering into personal pathology—and profits from managing it indefinitely.[34]

None of this is to deny that some people experience relief from antidepressants. Some do, and that matters. But helping some does not absolve a system that has oversold benefits, downplayed harms, obscured withdrawal effects, selectively published data, and resisted non-pharmacological care that cannot be patented or monetized.

A mental health system that cannot tolerate critique is not a healing system. An industry that profits from despair while denying its role in suicidality is not benevolent. And a culture that treats suicide as a chemical failure rather than a collective warning is avoiding the truth. People do not need to be fixed. They need safety, dignity, connection, justice, and reasons to live that go beyond symptom reduction.

Until Big Pharma and the systems aligned with it reckon honestly with what the research actually shows, and with what patients have been saying for decades, suicidality will continue to be treated as a side effect rather than a signal. And people will continue to suffer in silence, while the industry calls it care.

Black Box Warning and Side Effects

Did you know that all antidepressants are required by the FDA to have a Black Box warning? The most serious level of safety warning? This warning exists because antidepressants have been shown to increase the risk of suicidal thoughts and behaviors in children, adolescents, and young adults up to age twenty-five, particularly in the early stages of treatment or when doses are changed.[35] In some cases, individuals who were previously experiencing depression may develop new or intensified suicidal thinking after starting medication.

We are treating depression and anxiety with medications that increase the risk of suicidality and numb our feelings. Why in the world would this be the recommended course of action? Why, as parents and helpers, would we be trained that we should encourage our kids and families to get on medication to treat what is a product of our society and culture? Why do prescribing doctors not tell you this? The U.S. pharmaceutical industry is one of the most profitable industries in the history of the world, averaging a return of 17 percent on revenue over the last quarter century. Drug costs have been the most rapidly rising element in health care spending in recent years. Antidepressant medications rank third in pharmaceutical sales worldwide, with $13.4 billion in sales last year alone. This represents 4.2 percent of all pharmaceutical sales globally. Antipsychotic medications generated $6.5 billion in revenue.[36] This presents a difficult and often overlooked reality: Medications prescribed to treat depression can, in certain individuals and at certain points in treatment, increase the risk of suicide. This risk is why close monitoring is necessary, but often not highlighted during the initial weeks of treatment. Despite the known risks related to the Black Box warning, this information is not always fully understood or openly discussed. Medication is often presented as a primary or immediate solution, without equal emphasis on the complexity and potential risks involved, or on the broader context in which depression and anxiety arise. As a result, individuals and families may consent to treatment without fully grasping the importance of monitoring, support, and alternative or complementary approaches.

This is not to say that antidepressants should never be used. In some cases, they are helpful and life-saving. But it does call for a more nuanced and transparent conversation about their role. If a treatment designed to alleviate suffering can, in some cases, intensify it, then we must ask deeper questions about how we are approaching care.

Are we relying too heavily on medication as a solution to experiences that are also rooted in environment, disconnection, trauma, and loss of meaning? Are we equipping individuals with the support, awareness, and context needed to navigate both the benefits and the risks?

If we are to move toward a more humane and effective model of mental health care, we must hold two truths at once: Medication can reduce suffering and save lives in some situations, *and* it can also numb, increase dissociation, and increase vulnerability in ways that require careful attention, support, and broader understanding. That it is a tool for specific cases *and* it is being over prescribed to deal with depression induced by societal factors. That the overuse of antidepressants is a response to the socially constructed idea that we should not go through periods of depression. Only by acknowledging this complexity can we begin to build systems of care that are not only effective, but truly safe, transparent, and responsive to the full human experience.

CHAPTER 4:

Other Effective Treatments

The Gut & Nutrition

While we continue to treat depression with pharmaceuticals that are more than questionable, we seem to ignore the role of nutrition. In addition to our emotional environment, when addressing mental health, our internal physical environment needs to be considered. Contrary to the idea that serotonin is only a brain chemical, the majority of the body's serotonin (90 to 95 percent) is produced in the gastrointestinal tract by enterochromaffin cells and influenced by gut microbes. This serotonin plays roles in digestion, motility, appetite, sleep regulation, and mood signaling, and it participates in communication between the gut and brain via the gut—brain axis.[37]

Tryptophan, an essential amino acid found in protein-rich foods, is the precursor to serotonin. Nutritional factors, such as the balance of macronutrients and availability of key micronutrients (e.g., B vitamins, vitamin D, magnesium, and iron), affect the synthesis and regulation of serotonin and its related pathways.[38]

Serotonin is a key signal in the gut—brain axis, a bidirectional network linking the central nervous system (the brain and the gut). Signals from the gut, including microbial metabolites and neurotransmitters, influence brain function and emotional regulation, while brain-derived signals affect gut physiology. This communication occurs at least partly via the vagus nerve, a major neural highway between gut and brain. While gut-produced serotonin cannot directly cross the blood—brain barrier, it can influence brain processes indirectly through neural, immune, and endocrine-signaling pathways.[39]

Implications for Mood, Depression, and Mental Health

Emerging evidence links nutritional influences on gut serotonin and microbiota with mental health outcomes. Imbalances in the microbiome and disruptions in serotonin production have been associated with depression, anxiety, sleep disturbances, and other mood-related conditions, suggesting a multifaceted relationship between diet, gut ecology, and emotional well-being.

Additionally, deficiencies in vitamins B12, folate (B9), D, and minerals like magnesium and zinc, are strongly linked to increased risks of depression and anxiety. These nutrients are essential for regulating neurotransmitters (serotonin, dopamine), managing stress responses, and supporting brain function. Omega-3 fatty acids and iron are also critical for mood stability.[40]

While we can easily turn this knowledge into another formal, pharmaceutical intervention, I encourage deeper critical thinking. Why is it that our nutrition has such an impact on our gut microbiome and subsequent mental health? What has changed about our connection to our food sources? The lack of connection to our land and animals seems to play a significant role in our increasing mental health issues. Addressing this issue may seem harder or more complex than prescribing a medication to treat the gut, but if we do not look to root causes, we are continuing to engage in a vicious cycle of treating the fallout from our own creation.

Dissociation & Ketamine

Dissociation is a pathologized condition in the Diagnostic Statistics Manual, and it is also experienced on a spectrum. Many people exist in a perpetual state of disconnection who may not meet the diagnostic criteria to be labeled as "dissociated." As seen in the figure below, we are currently addressing feelings of disconnection that lead to diagnosis of depression or anxiety with medication. Anti-depressant medication often leads to a numbing

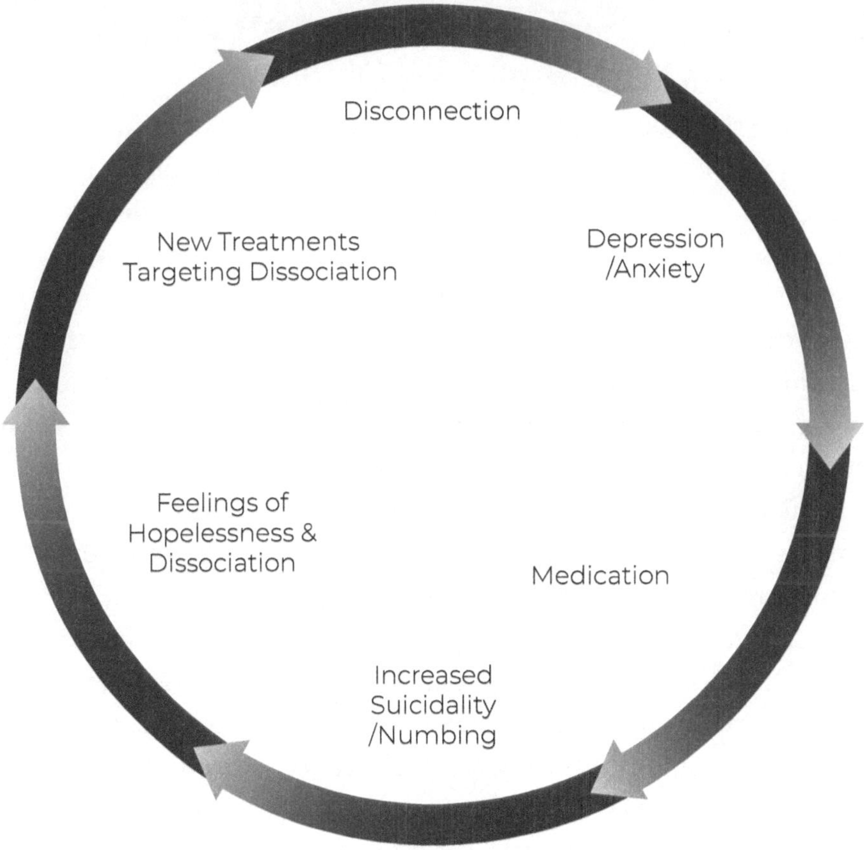

effect, reducing negative feelings, but at the same time reducing intensity of all feelings—including the positive ones. As we know, medications can also lead to suicidality. These side effects can lead to a feeling of hopelessness and the nervous system's protective mechanism of further dissociation.

In a society where many individuals are already living in states of chronic disconnection and dissociation, this may be part of why ketamine works so well. In some ways, this mirrors a principle seen in homeopathy (a 200-year-old alternative medical system based on "like cures like"—substances causing symptoms can treat them). When dissociation is widespread, manifesting as numbness, disconnection, and an inability to fully feel, introducing a controlled, therapeutic dissociative state may help interrupt and reorganize those patterns. However, this is where we must be careful not to miss the deeper truth.

While this book explores the need to approach mental and emotional health through a holistic lens, it is essential to hold a *both/and* perspective. There are individuals who are deeply suffering—many experiencing severe depression and active suicidality—and they require immediate, effective intervention. Not everyone has access to, or is ready for, a paradigm that integrates meaning, embodiment, and the full human experience. Some are in crisis. And in those moments, our responsibility is clear: We must reduce suffering and keep people alive.

One of the most promising treatments emerging to meet this need is ketamine. Research has shown that ketamine can rapidly reduce suicidal ideation and symptoms of treatment-resistant depression—often within hours rather than weeks. Unlike traditional antidepressants that primarily target serotonin, ketamine acts on the glutamate system, increasing synaptic connectivity and promoting neuroplasticity. In doing so, it appears to help "reset" brain circuits impacted by chronic stress and depression. Importantly, ketamine does not carry the same increased risk of suicidality seen in some antidepressants—in fact, it has been shown to decrease suicidal thoughts in the short term, making it an invaluable tool in crisis care.

Ketamine has a long clinical history. Since the 1970s, it has been used safely as an anesthetic in both human and veterinary medicine. In 2019, the FDA approved a Ketamine-based treatment (esketamine) for treatment-resistant depression, administered under medical supervision in certified settings. While it carries some risk of misuse and psychological dependence, its controlled clinical use has opened a new frontier in treating severe mental health conditions.[41]

And yet, an important question remains: Why is Ketamine so effective right now?

One emerging perspective points to its dissociative properties. Ketamine induces an altered state of consciousness, loosening rigid thought patterns, softening identity structures, and shifting perception. Ketamine can be highly effective at alleviating symptoms, particularly in the short term. It can interrupt suicidality, create space, and provide relief where other treatments have failed. Traditional antidepressant pharmaceuticals may offer a numbing quality, but they do not create an emotional environment where the deeper work can be accessed. Ketamine creates emotional space and offers resourcing that can accommodate entering into the deep work. But if we rely on it as the primary or sole solution or use it to feel better or bypass pain that is present and needs to be fully felt and worked through, we risk continuing a pattern that has defined much of modern mental health care: treating the symptoms of a problem without addressing its root cause.[42]

If widespread depression, anxiety, and suicidality are, at least in part, connected to chronic disconnection from self, from others, from community, and from meaning, then no pharmacological intervention alone can fully resolve them. Ketamine can open a window, and what fills that window matters.

We must ask:

- What happens after the relief?
- What supports are in place to help individuals integrate what they experience?
- How do we address the underlying conditions that led them there in the first place?

There is much to learn from Indigenous and community-based approaches to emotional suffering, which often do not separate grief, depression, anxiety, and suicidality into isolated categories. Instead, they recognize a shared root: disconnection, lack of expression, lack of witnessing, and absence of communal support. Healing, in these contexts, involves not only the individual, but the collective, through ritual, storytelling, presence, and relationship.

In contrast, our current paradigm has become narrow and fragmented, focusing heavily on brain chemistry (medication) and cognitive coping (therapy), while often overlooking the broader human experience. The idea that depression is solely a biological disorder has been increasingly challenged. While biology plays a role, it is not the whole story.

The invitation, then, is not to reject treatments like Ketamine, but to place them within a larger, more complete framework. We need systems that can both:

- Stabilize individuals in crisis, using tools like Ketamine when necessary *and*
- Support long-term healing through connection, embodiment, meaning-making, and community.

Ketamine may help someone step out of the most acute layer of suffering. But if we do not address the deeper disconnection beneath it, we will continue to cycle through relief without resolution.

Opposing Cycle of Resourcing & Connection

If dissociation is a nervous system response that causes separation when we do not feel resourced to feel fully, then nervous system resourcing is a large part of the answer for how we begin to live more fully connected to and in our bodies as well as how we engage with others. While the dissociation cycle image depicts a negative feedback loop, we must also look at the opposing positive feedback loop. When our nervous systems feel resourced through stillness, presence, connection, support, and witnessing, we are able to live more fully in our bodies. Stillness and presence are required to genuinely connect with all of the parts of ourselves and with others. When we have genuine connection, we begin to feel supported, witnessed, and seen. Once we experience the benefits of this foundational layer of connection, we begin to feel hope. Hope, in combination with connection, leads to joy—and joy allows us to enter into deeper layers of connection. This positive ripple effect is the antidote to the cycle of disconnection and dissociation in which our society has found itself.

Plant Allies

Unlike pharmaceutical anti-depressant medication, plant allies tend to help us fully feel and see—uncovering the root of our distress. While plant medicine is not readily accessible or even legal in many states, as pharmaceuticals are, they provide an alternative treatment that is highly effective and has fewer side effects. As of this writing, the Federal government has fast tracked research and expansion of psychedelic medicine, specifically for use with veterans and those with trauma. While LSD, DMT, Iboga, and many other psychedelics are still in the early stages of research studies on their positive effects on mental health, and MDMA has decades of research to support future legalization, psilocybin is currently the only one to be legalized in some states for therapeutic use based on research that suggests it may be an effective treatment for depression and anxiety among other potential pathologies. Clinical trials have shown that moderate to high doses of psilocybin, combined with psychological support, can lead to significant and sometimes long-lasting reductions in depressive symptoms and anxiety, including in individuals with treatment-resistant depression. Participants often report improvements in mood, emotional processing, and overall well-being following guided sessions.[43]

Psilocybin treatment has been shown to be generally well tolerated. Common acute effects include nausea, dizziness, increased heart rate, and temporary anxiety or confusion as the drug takes effect. Some individuals may experience intense emotional reactions or psychological distress during the session, which is why therapeutic support is typically provided and highly recommended. In rare cases, psilocybin may exacerbate underlying mental health conditions, such as psychosis in vulnerable individuals. Most side effects are short-lived and resolve within hours.[44]

In everyday life, the brain's communication networks (specifically the Default Mode Network) settle into rigid, predictable patterns. Think of the snowflakes lying quietly at the bottom of a globe. This can be great for daily routines, but it can also trap people in repetitive, negative thought loops (like chronic depression, anxiety, or addiction). When a psychedelic is introduced, it temporarily "shakes the globe." Normal, entrenched pathways of thinking are disrupted, and different regions of the brain begin communicating in unconstrained, chaotic ways. As the medicine wears off, the "snow" slowly settles, but it forms new, healthier drifts. This period immediately following the experience is often called the "afterglow," characterized by increased mental flexibility, neuroplasticity, and emotional openness. Many psychedelics allow for neuroplasticity to remain for two weeks to one month after the treatment. This window of opportunity allows new ways of perceiving challenges, increased positive mood, decreased anxiety, and increased sense of social connection to take hold. This window of opportunity, especially when including a trained guide for integration, allows new ways of perceiving challenges to take hold, such as: increased positive mood, decreased anxiety, increased sense of social connection, and spiritual/mystical insights impacting the way people engage with and understand the world and their place in it.[45]

CHAPTER 5:

Post-Traumatic Growth, Gratitude, Joy & Hope

"You can do it like it's a great weight, or you can do it like it's part of the dance." —Ram Dass, *Be Here Now*

Issues with pharmaceuticals and pathologizing the human experience with the DSM aside, one of the larger issues to be considered is that we are not fully utilizing the opportunities for post traumatic growth (Layer 2). It is within the deeper work, where suffering is not only relieved but integrated, that post-traumatic growth and gratitude begin to emerge, not as forced positivity, but as meaningful responses to having fully lived through and learned from our most difficult experiences.

While the idea of Post-Traumatic Growth (PTG) has arguably been the basis for many spiritual practice for millennia, it first emerged in the academic world in the mid-1990s through the work of Tedeschi and Calhoun, and over time the model has continued to evolve and become more detailed. PTG is described as the positive psychological changes that can happen when someone struggles through trauma or a deeply challenging life experience. Many peer reviewed academic studies have shown the existence and implications of PTG. It is a hopeful, meaning centered, framework that orients individuals and mental health practitioners toward a strengths-based and meaning-centered approach for those who have experienced a trauma.[46]

What's important here is that PTG doesn't replace the painful outcomes of trauma—it exists alongside them. In other words, growth and pain can happen at the same time. Post-traumatic growth can show up as shifts in how a person sees themselves, how they relate to others, and how they understand life. This might include greater self-awareness and confidence, deeper relationships, more openness and compassion, a stronger appreciation for life, and even discovering new possibilities or directions after hardship. These are the opposing opportunities in Layer 4 (ego). PTG allows for the ego to respond to hardship with adaptive strategies like using perspective, using reflective solitude, becoming in touch with spirituality, using imagination to create a safe internal world, and then being able to experience joy, humor, and creative expression.[47]

On some level, people have always understood that both positive and negative life experiences can change us. But historically, especially in psychiatry and clinical research, the focus has been much more on how trauma contributes to mental illness—how it can trigger, worsen, or shape psychological symptoms and long-term mental health outcomes. Trauma became a central concept in understanding psychopathology and illness trajectories. What received far less attention, until more recently, is the reality that trauma can also sometimes lead to meaningful growth—not instead of the pain, but through the process of surviving and living with it. Post-traumatic growth often leads one to find deep meaning to life, death, and the suffering and joy in between.[48]

But not everyone who experiences trauma experiences post-traumatic growth. Why is this? We come back to creating capacity. When someone is not internally and externally resourced and supported, they are often not resilient enough to emerge from the ashes to explore their inner world and ultimately find meaning. Resilience isn't cultivated in isolation—it requires community, support, being held, and true unconditional connection.

The frame in which we operate as parents, mental health providers, doctors, educators, and leaders needs to be one in which we see it as a window of opportunity for learning and expansion instead of running away from or trying to numb the impact of trauma. As leaders, we must recognize the need to create supportive environments and containers that can hold and allow for one to feel safe enough to engage in the PTG process. An initial and critical component of this safety is to first understand the process of meaning-making through the Human Experience Labyrinth. When one can identify where they are and what pieces they must move through, it provides a normalized path. It provides somewhere to begin, and a knowing that forward movement is possible.[49]

Gratitude, Joy & Hope

Gratitude, from a scientific perspective, is not simply a positive emotion but a measurable neurobiological and psychological process that shapes how we perceive and respond to the world. Research shows that practicing gratitude activates the prefrontal cortex, enhances dopamine and serotonin production, and reduces activity in the amygdala, supporting emotional regulation, resilience, and overall well-being. It has also been linked to improved sleep, reduced stress and inflammation, and stronger relational bonds.

Within a post pathology Human Experience Labyrinth orientation, however, gratitude is not about bypassing pain or forcing positivity. Instead, it emerges through meaning-making, through our willingness to engage with the full spectrum of human experience, including suffering. When we hold both truths, that life can be difficult and that something meaningful can still be found within it, gratitude becomes less about what is "good" and more about what is real, present, and formative. Over time, this deepens into a more mature form of gratitude: not only appreciating moments of ease, but also recognizing the lessons, growth, and transformation that come from the hardest experiences of our lives. This does not mean we are grateful *for* suffering in a simplistic or dismissive way, but that we can, in time, hold a sense of gratitude for what those experiences have revealed, shaped, or awakened within us, allowing even our most difficult moments to become part of a meaningful and integrated life.

When we feel a deep sense of meaning and gratitude for all that life has to offer us, we are able to access hope and joy. When we are free from needing our lives to be a certain way, we are able to experience the joy that naturally arises from gratitude—gratitude for the complexity and duality of life that has shown us who we are and pointed us toward meaning. We find hope in the knowing that we can experience the full spectrum of emotion and that the very experience is what will lead us toward joy. And we find joy in finding and experiencing alignment and meaning. When we experience alignment and meaning, we finally know our true selves—and knowing our true selves is bliss. So, while we must experience the duality, ultimately, as we have experienced the depths of all types of emotions, the harshness of duality fades and we are free in knowing our full selves. In this way, the definition of joy might be different than what is commonplace. It is hard to put into words, and to truly know it, one must feel the nuance of it in the body. My best attempt at encapsulating joy in writing, is the ecstasy of feeling all of creation, in full presence. The euphoria and exhilaration that comes from being fully immersed and present to the cycle of birth, growth, death, and transformation.

CHAPTER 6:

Psychotherapy & Psychoeducation

We've covered the medication side of our current treatment model. Let's now turn toward therapy. Therapy largely falls into Layer 4 of the Human Experience Labyrinth. It is helpful to manage how we engage in life, but its main use is to gain control of our ego's response to trauma and hardship. It is generally in fifty-minute increments and limited by the number of sessions allowed by insurance, or it is not covered at all and patients must pay out-of-pocket. It is often our first line of defense when experiencing a crisis—emotional first aid, if you will. We rely on a single person with a single cultural background and experience (possibly not your own, especially if you are a minority) who was trained in generalist mental health (and who is hopefully but not guaranteed to be working on their own mental health alongside you) to know how to help us in our complicated stories that include physical, emotional, structural, ancestral, and relational needs. The pressure put on this treatment to "fix" the client's issue is unrealistic and unfair to both the practitioner and to the client.

There are many interventions used with varying purposes, as seen in the chart on the next page. As you can see in the "primary target/purpose" column, the interventions target the underlying thoughts, emotions, behaviors, and relational patterns that maintain psychological distress, helping individuals reduce symptoms, build coping skills, process trauma, and improve functioning.

Reduction of symptoms and distress is important when they pose a potential harm to themselves or others. Otherwise, the symptoms and distress are the very things that can teach us, and trying mute them inadvertently takes away the very catalyst we need for Post-Traumatic Growth. It is highly uncomfortable and sometimes scary to witness or to be the one suffering—it makes sense that we want to remedy it as soon as possible. There is a line of thought around resistance, and leaning into that is important to note here. When we resist, often what we are resisting becomes stronger. When we lean in and surrender, the thing that is causing us suffering tends to soften. What would it look like if we leaned into the challenging emotions, allowing ourselves to fully feel and experience them? Would they begin to dissipate?

Resistance vs. Acceptance Exercise:

1. Take a moment to notice your body at a baseline state.
2. Now, think to yourself that whatever you have been struggling with in your life should not be—your anxiety, depression, fear, etc. They don't belong in your life and need to be removed as quickly as possible. Notice your body now. What do you feel?
3. Clear that energy and attempt to move back to your baseline state.
4. Now, think to yourself that whatever you are struggling with in life is real, it belongs in this moment, you can feel it and know that it won't be there forever, and you know that it is just a normal part of your human experience. Notice your body now. What do you feel?

Depression and anxiety are often due to a circumstance. We need the signal of these emotions to let us know that something needs to change. We need to fully feel and process in order to make the changes necessary. Building coping skills to move through the challenges of life is also important, as we can't do the deeper emotional work unless we have resourced and regulated nervous systems.

Below is a chart offering an overview of the main evidence-based mental health interventions, by condition, outlining its primary target or purpose.

Evidence-Based/Informed Mental Health Interventions by Condition

Condition	Intervention	Primary Target/Purpose
Depression	Cognitive Behavioral Therapy (CBT)	Restructure negative thought patterns; reduce depressive symptoms[50]
	Behavioral Activation (BA)	Increase engagement in rewarding activities; reduce withdrawal[51]
	Interpersonal Therapy (IPT)	Improve relationship functioning; address grief/role transitions
	Mindfulness-Based Cognitive Therapy (MBCT)	Prevent depressive relapse; build awareness of thought patterns
	Acceptance & Commitment Therapy (ACT)	Increase psychological flexibility; reduce experiential avoidance[52]
Anxiety Disorders (GAD, Social Anxiety, Panic, Phobias)	Cognitive Behavioral Therapy (CBT)	Reduce cognitive distortions; build coping skills[53]
	Exposure Therapy	Reduce fear response through gradual, repeated exposure[54]
	Acceptance Based Therapy (ACT)	Reduce avoidance; increase values-based action despite anxiety[55]
	Mindfulness Based Cognitive Therapy (MBCT)	Improve emotion regulation and reduce rumination[56]
PTSD / Trauma-Related Disorders	Prolonged Exposure (PE)	Reduce trauma-related fear through structured exposure
	EMDR	Reprocess traumatic memories to reduce distress[57]
	Trauma-Focused CBT (TF-CBT)	Cognitive restructuring and trauma processing (often used with youth)

	CPT (Cognitive Processing Therapy) Adventure/Nature Based Therapy	Restructure trauma-related beliefs (guilt, shame, safety)[58] Substance abuse issues, effective in improving self-confidence, emotional regulation, and resilience[59]
Borderline Personality Disorder (BPD)	Dialectical Behavior Therapy (DBT)	Emotion regulation; reduce self-harm and suicidality[60]
Substance Use Disorders	Motivational Interviewing (MI)	Increase readiness for change; resolve ambivalence[61]
	CBT for Substance Use	Identify triggers; develop relapse prevention skills
Obsessive-Compulsive Disorder (OCD)	Exposure and Response Prevention (ERP)	Reduce compulsions by preventing ritual behaviors during exposure
Eating Disorders	CBT-E (Enhanced CBT)	Normalize eating patterns; address distorted beliefs about weight/shape
Bipolar Disorder	Psychoeducation + CBT	Improve medication adherence; identify early warning signs
Relapse Prevention (Across Conditions)	MBCT	Reduce recurrence of depression
	DBT Skills Training	Improve long-term emotion regulation

Interventions used by therapists are largely evidence-based; however, the evidence base is usually based on studies that aim to alleviate symptoms and include an overrepresentation of White participants and have an underrepresentation of marginalized groups; racial and ethnic minorities, individuals with low socioeconomic status, sexual minorities, and rural populations are consistently underrepresented in research. As these evidence-based or informed therapies do not reflect the diverse cultures and backgrounds that are present in therapy, there are serious concerns about their application to these populations with unique cultural considerations.

Therapists are generally trained in a handful of these approaches, but certainly it is not feasible to be an expert in all of them. The studies that have been done on therapies deemed "evidence-based" are helping. Many people report some benefit from therapy. Therapy helps the brain understand why the ego (personality or nervous system) is responding to life circumstances the way that it is and gives us language and skills to respond to and/or perceive our experiences in different ways. Instead of a focus on finding meaning in our lives, it largely focuses on how to find equilibrium and skills to engage in life with a more self-reflective and self-aware approach.

Therapists are trained in how to effectively interact with clients and deliver interventions; however, what is often ignored (out of necessity because of the already existing shortage of mental health practitioners) is the importance of the client being able to identify with the therapist in race, gender, age, and experience. Currently, in the United States, the field lacks diversity, with 83 to 86 percent of psychologists and 88 percent of counselors identifying as White. Only about 10.4 percent of psychiatrists are Black, Hispanic, or Native American.[62] The workforce is heavily female, with women making up 78.4 percent of counselors and over 70 percent of therapists. Additionally, the prevalence of personal trauma history ranged from 19 to 81 percent.[63]

While therapy creates an opportunity for human connection, witnessing, and understanding—albeit transactional and generally infrequent due to cost and availability—it is critical for clients to gain wisdom from someone who has personal experience that can translate to the client's life. While a client may be able to learn coping skills or process what they are going through, the deeper work is most effective when it comes from someone who has gone through and continues to do their own processing work. I am not proposing that therapy be taken out of the mix; it most definitely has a place in navigating our human experience. But again, I am proposing that we zoom out to consider the entire picture and not place such a heavy emphasis on therapy as *the* solution.

There are new approaches to therapy that seem promising and are transpersonal in nature. Internal Family Systems, Psychedelic Assisted Therapy, and Certified Spiritually Informed Therapists take into account the many layers of the human experience and attempt to incorporate them into their 1:1, paid sessions. This is a helpful step in the right direction; however, barriers to access are still relevant and we are not fully incorporating the relations Layer (4). We must catch ourselves when we see a new, shiny therapeutic approach as "the answer" and become fixated on just one layer of the human experience.

The quote below by Viktor Frankl calls on us to use duality (opposing feelings/experiences) as a means for moving through the human experience instead of giving up. It highlights the importance of using all of the layers in the psychotherapeutic and psychoeducational space—integrating all pieces of the Labyrinth into our deep therapeutic work. True transformation comes from diving into and incorporating each layer of the Labyrinth.

> "Thus it can be seen that mental health is based on a certain degree of tension. ... Such a tension is inherent in the human being and therefore is indispensable to mental well-being. ... I consider it a dangerous misconception of mental hygiene to assume that what man needs in the first place is equilibrium or, as it is called in biology, "homeostasis," i.e., a tensionless state. What man actually needs is not a tensionless state but rather the striving and struggling for a worthwhile goal, a freely chosen task. ... So if therapists wish to foster their patients' mental health, they should not be afraid to create a sound amount of tension through a reorientation toward the meaning of one's life." —Viktor Frankl, *Man's Search For Meaning*[64]

The System is Falling Apart

Something new cannot be built until the old begins to fall apart. We are living in the midst of that unraveling—a collective reckoning with how we have come to understand and respond to the human experience. The long-held tendency to pathologize what is, in many ways, a natural and predictable response to life's conditions is no longer resonating in the same way. There is a growing awareness that methods we have relied on—medication, traditional therapy models, or individualized notions of "self-care"—are not sufficient on its own to address the depth and complexity of human suffering.

We are beginning to see the limits of approaches that isolate the individual from their environment, or that attempt to resolve distress without fully understanding its roots. The conditions that shape our lives—our relationships, communities, cultural systems, and broader societal structures—cannot be separated from our internal experiences. A more complete vision of mental health must account for both the inner and outer worlds, expanding beyond what has traditionally been considered within the scope of care. Without this, many of our current solutions risk becoming temporary measures—relieving pressure in the moment, but failing to address what lies beneath.

The chapters that follow are dedicated to reimagining this landscape. They offer a reorientation toward the Human Experience Labyrinth as a framework for understanding and engaging with the fullness of being human. This is not simply a shift in practice, but a shift in language, perspective, and relationship—to ourselves, to one another, and to the systems we are part of. It is also, in many ways, a return to something we have known before: the importance of community, of shared experience, and of being witnessed and supported within it.

As a mental health professional, I have come to understand my role not as something to preserve, but ultimately to transcend. The goal is not to create lifelong dependency on systems of care, but to support individuals and communities in reclaiming their own capacity to navigate life, to find meaning, and to support one another. In a post pathology orientation where relationship, context, and shared humanity are centered, it is possible to imagine a future where care becomes less transactional, more accessible, and more deeply integrated into everyday life.

Without this kind of shift, we risk continuing to operate from places of unprocessed and unintegrated experience. When wounds remain unacknowledged, they do not disappear—they are carried forward, often expressed outwardly in ways that shape our relationships, our communities, and the world around us. Healing, then, is not only personal—it is collective. As we begin to tend to what lives within us, we also begin to transform what exists between us.

> "There are no weapons more dangerous than our wounds." —Andrea Gibson, *Take Me With You*[65]

SECTION III:

New Paradigm

Shedding Light on the Core of the Labyrinth

"Love goes very far beyond the physical person of the beloved. It finds its deepest meaning in his spiritual being, his inner self. Whether or not he is actually present, whether or not his is still alive at all, ceases somehow to be of importance." —Viktor Frankl, *Man's Search for Meaning*

Much of modern life is structured around repetition and maintenance—patterns that prioritize productivity and survival, but often leave little room for depth, expression, or connection. Sleep, eat, work, watch TV or scroll, repeat. We go through the motions of life unconsciously. While these rhythms can provide stability, they can also quietly shape a life that feels distracted and disconnected from meaning. Over time, this disconnection does not always present as a crisis, but as something more subtle: a flattening of experience, a sense of going through the motions, or an undercurrent of restlessness that is difficult to name.

Human beings are not wired for mere maintenance. There is an inherent pull toward creation, contribution, connection, and expression. When these aspects of ourselves are consistently underdeveloped or unsupported by our environments, the impact accumulates. What emerges is not necessarily dysfunction, but a quiet misalignment, a signal that something essential is not being engaged.

This becomes more visible when life introduces disruption (Layer 2). Experiences such as loss, illness, or transition often ask us to reorganize how we understand ourselves and the world around us. Without a broader context to hold these experiences, they can feel disorienting or overwhelming, not simply because of their intensity, but because there is no clear way to integrate them into a larger sense of meaning.

One way to understand this is through the image of a puzzle. Life continuously offers pieces—some expected, others not. Without a sense of the larger picture, each new piece can feel random or burdensome. What the Human Experience Labyrinth offers is not a fixed answer, but a way of orienting to the whole—an understanding that allows each experience, even the most difficult ones, to be placed within a broader context of becoming.

This shift in orientation also invites a reconsideration of how support is offered. Much of the helping field has been shaped around the goal of resolving problems, often under pressure to produce timely and measurable outcomes. While this has its place, it can also narrow the scope of what is considered meaningful care. When the focus moves away from fixing and toward understanding, different questions begin to emerge, questions that open space for connection, reflection, and ongoing development rather than immediate resolution.

In this section, we turn more fully toward the inner layers of the Human Experience Labyrinth, where this kind of engagement becomes possible. The earlier layers—those shaped by duality, fear, and common human suffering, along with the opportunity for post-traumatic growth—remain foundational; however, they are not where the most dynamic movement occurs. They describe the conditions of being human, but not the full range of how we can relate to those conditions.

As individuals encounter these outer layers, the initial response is often to manage and stabilize—to make sense of reactions, regulate emotions, and develop ways of coping. This is reflected in what we understand as ego structures and nervous system responses. While this work is essential, it is not the endpoint. It marks the beginning of a deeper process, one that invites movement beyond management and into exploration, awareness, and integration.

The chapters that follow will focus on these inner dimensions, where the work shifts from reacting to experience toward relating to it differently. It is here that the core of the Labyrinth becomes more visible, not as something to reach, but as something to engage with, again and again, as part of a continually unfolding human experience. The first two layers (duality and fear, common human suffering experiences) are not discussed in depth as they are set experiences and are not where the creative engagement, movement, and reimagination in the Labyrinth live.

Once one has a perspective shift, and can orient themselves toward meaning making instead of Why Me?, the outer two layers become less pronounced. Most day to day living happens in the relational field (Layer 4). Disconnection from any of the various relationships we have in life leads to despair, depression, anxiety, and addiction. Cultivating connection in all of the ways we can, is the work that builds resilience and hope. Each day, we would benefit from building opportunities for each type of connection into our routine. When we have a solid foundation of connection (in all of our relationships—physical, mental, emotional, spiritual, and with community, ancestors, and the earth), we are resourced, regulated, and can find gratitude and joy more easily. This centering in connection allows us to spend our energy on fulfilling our purpose through service.

CHAPTER 7:

Reimagining Ego Management

As we move through the outer layers of the human experience, those shaped by duality, fear, and common forms of suffering, we begin to internalize a particular belief that we are alone in what we are experiencing and that it is our responsibility to fix it. This assumption naturally shapes how we respond to distress, both individually and within systems of care. The initial approach often becomes one of management—working to regulate, control, or make sense of our reactions through the lens of the ego. This is reflected in what we might consider the third layer of the Labyrinth: ego and nervous system regulation.

The traditional method for engaging this layer is therapy. As discussed earlier, therapy serves an important role in helping individuals navigate life. Broadly, it tends to focus on two primary aims: first, identifying solutions to problems or reactions to specific experiences, and second, exploring the underlying reasons for those reactions through deeper psychoanalysis. This process is largely centered on the story—what happened, how it impacted us, and how we came to respond in the ways that we do. And yet, the story is only part of the experience. What about the shame that lingers beneath it? The fear that shapes it? The need for forgiveness, both of self and others, that often remains unspoken? The larger existential questions about who we are and why we're here?

While psychotherapy can be effective in helping us understand and regulate our responses, it can also stop short of fully engaging the deeper layers of what it means to feel. When the focus remains primarily on making sense of experience or building coping skills, we risk bypassing the opportunity to actually move through the emotional and energetic reality of what is present.

What if, in addition to understanding and managing our responses, we began to approach them as teachers? Each ego reaction, whether it shows up as darkness, clinging, desire, ignorance, excess, forgetting, resistance to the body, or rage, contains within it the possibility of its opposite. These experiences are not simply problems to be resolved, but invitations to expand our awareness. When met with curiosity rather than judgment, they create opportunities to experience humor in darkness, perspective in clinging, imagination in ignorance, stillness in excess, remembrance through creative expression, spiritual connection through the body, and even joy alongside anger.

From this perspective, the goal is not simply to feel better or to understand why we feel the way we do. It is to more fully experience what it means to be human. Our very normal and predictable ego responses are not evidence that something is wrong with us; they are part of the process through which we come to know ourselves more deeply. In learning to hold both the light and the dark within us, we begin to move beyond managing the ego and into a more integrated relationship with it; one that allows for growth, awareness, and a fuller expression of who we are.

Layer 3 is where the malleable parts of the Labyrinth begin. Michael Singer's *The Untethered Soul* and Eckhart Tolle's *The Power of Now* are both seminal texts on identifying the ego as separate from the "self." Can we be curious and zoom out enough to see the ego (our personality) with wonder? When we can see the separation of our personality and coping skills from our "true self," we can then see that focusing our efforts on the ego is focusing on the parts of ourselves that are false, or not "true." While we do need to manage the very present ego, we are missing the boat if that is where we stop.

We can clearly see how the role of duality helps us to work within our egos. When a challenging part of our ego emerges, we have the opportunity to also experience its opposite. This duality within ego is a critical component to learning more about our true self and developing the continual self-inquiry muscle. Below, I outline the lessons we can learn from the "dark" parts of the ego (also seen as sins in religious contexts) and the opposing "light" side. Inspired by Meggan Watterson's take on reimagining the seven deadly sins as seven divine embodied powers,[66] I'd like to introduce the idea of "sin" merely being a divinely-inspired emotion for expansion. What if the "sins" (common human emotions/responses) exist in order for us to fully know ourselves and be in full expression?

When we suppress emotions because we see them as "bad" or "dark," we don't allow them to move through us so that we can experience their opposite. This suppression creates dis-ease, physically, mentally, and emotionally. This suppression is in large part what contributes to a dissociated society. When mental health professionals are working with ego structures, this can be a helpful framework to fully explore and feel, rather than to fix.

Egoic Expressions vs. the Opposing Embodied Powers

Egoic (Sin) Expression	Opposing Embodied Powers
Darkness	Humor
Clinging/Desire	Relativity
Ignorance	Imagination
Excess	Solitude
Forgetting	Creative Expression
The Body	Spirituality
Rage	Joy

Darkness: Humor

When everything goes dark and quiet, it can feel like love and light has left. But in that silence, your inner light has the opportunity to awaken. Even when the outer world fades, your inner light remains. When you are feeling overwhelming darkness, it is helpful to utilize the opposing force of humor. Humor can lighten dark and heavy emotions.

Clinging/desire: Relativity

The ego holds on to what it can't control: people, outcomes, the past. The soul asks us to release and trust the unfolding. When we cling and desire, we are given the opportunity to zoom out and find relativity. When we see things relatively, we see the larger vision for life and humanity. Things come and go. Nothing stays the same. When things or people leave, other things or people will enter into our lives.

Ignorance: Imagination

Ignorance is forgetting who we are beneath the masks, beneath the personality of the ego. When we stop performing, truth appears. Admitting our ignorance lets us see beyond illusion. We can use imagination to see beyond the illusion. When our imagination is sparked, we see all possibilities, all realities. We can create our own realities. Whatever we experience in our minds is a real experience. Imagination allows for expansion and remembering that we are limitless.

Excess: Solitude

We overdo and overfill because something inside aches to be soothed. The way back is love—remembering we're sacred, not for what we do or have, but for who we are. When we consume excess—energy, people, things, work, food, activities, etc.—we provide ourselves an opportunity to experience the opposite: solitude. Solitude allows us the space and stillness to remember who we are beyond the ego. It allows us to connect with our true nature.

Forgetting: Creative Expression

We forget we are more than fear, more than flesh—that we actually do not originate from duality, but are connected as part of something greater. Creative expression allows us to remember our true self through song, painting, dance, writing, playfulness ... when we create opportunities in our life to remember through our creative expression, we heal the part of us that feels separate and alone. Creativity = openness.

> "As the inner life of the prisoner tended to become more intense, he also experienced the beauty of art and nature as never before. Under their influence he sometimes even forgot his own frightful circumstances. If someone had seen our faces on the journey from Auschwitz to a Bavarian camp as we beheld the mountains of Salzburg with their summits glowing in the sunset, through the little barred windows of the prison carriage, he would never have believed that those were the faces of men who had given up all hope of life and liberty. Despite that factor—or maybe because of it—we were carried away by nature's beauty, which we had missed for so long." —Viktor Frankl, *Man's Search for Meaning*

The Body: Spirituality

The body isn't the obstacle; it's the guide. It carries wisdom and truth. We are invited to return to it with reverence. At times, we can become overidentified with the body. We feel we are a slave to its biology, weaknesses, and automatic reactions. While we are, in fact, in physical bodies, we can find relief from our overidentification when we turn to spirituality. Knowing that we are our bodies—*and* that we are *more* than our bodies—allows us to feel the full spectrum of our human experience as souls in human bodies.

> "The majority of prisoners suffered from a kind of inferiority complex. We all had once been or had fancied ourselves to be 'somebody.' Now we were treated like complete nonentities. (The consciousness of one's inner value is anchored in higher, more spiritual things, and cannot be shaken by camp life. But how many free men, let alone prisoners, possess it?)" —Viktor Frankl, *Man's Search for Meaning*

Rage: Joy

Anger, when honored, becomes clarity. Sacred rage protects what's true; destructive rage silences it. Even fire can be holy when guided by love. While rage can be a useful tool, staying stuck in that emotion can be harmful to both the individual experiencing it and those around them. The anecdote to rage is joy. We cannot fully know what joy is until we have experienced rage and despair. Intentionally creating awareness of the importance of joy and opportunities to experience more of it, can co-exist alongside feelings of anger. We must make room for both of them to exist.

We often enter into traditional therapy because we want to stop or relieve whatever it is that we are feeling or experiencing. There is a paradox within this framework of therapy—when we place a heavy focus on and resistance to what we are trying to alleviate, it actually strengthens and can feel more pronounced. Once we lean in, fully feel and experience, it often begins to dissipate. We can use these ego opportunities to lean in, feel, and then ultimately have room to truly know their opposite.

Spirituality & Therapy

There are several therapeutic approaches and tools focused on ego management that are now incorporating spirituality.

1. Internal Family Systems Therapy is an approach that identifies different parts of the ego and separates them out from the "true self." Many practitioners are now integrating spirituality into this approach; as one delves into what the "true self" means, the exploration inherently turns toward who we are, beyond our minds and bodies.
2. Dialectical Behavior Therapy focuses on teaching mindfulness, distress tolerance, emotion regulation, and interpersonal effectiveness through individual therapy, skills groups, and coaching. While not overtly spiritual, the

focus on mindfulness and nervous system regulation lends itself to exploration beyond the ego self.

3. Soul Work[67] identifies concepts to stabilize the mind, plant ideas, and lay the foundation for deeper, existential work. Similar to the purpose of the Human Experience Labyrinth, Soul Work is intended to help people move through challenging circumstances by understanding how the following concepts can help them move through life with greater clarity:
   a. Suffering
   b. Connecting With our Innate Wisdom
   c. Control
   d. Fear
   e. Post-Traumatic Growth
   f. Listening, Leaning In, and Softening
   g. Stillness
   h. Presence
   i. Non-attachment
   j. Perspective
   k. Acceptance
   l. Consciousness Studies
   m. Lessons from Nature
   n. Processing and Integration

While it is promising that traditional ego-oriented therapies are now incorporating components of spirituality and somatic awareness, we want to avoid becoming frozen on one side of the pendulum swing. We need to understand how to be in our bodies and work with our brains, while at the same time addressing the fullness of our human experience beyond just the body and brain. At the same time, we must be mindful of not attempting to be palatable to all approaches by staying in the middle—partially exploring the body and brain, and partially exploring the "true self." We need to be cognizant of fully exploring both. By staying in the middle or swinging to one side and staying there, we miss the full exploration and work. The goal is to seamlessly flow between the body, brain, *and* spiritual parts of self exploration and growth.

Practical Application

Individuals

Within the Human Experience Labyrinth, Layer 3 represents ego structures—the personality patterns, beliefs, and coping strategies we develop to navigate life. Rather than something to conquer, the ego is best understood as a protective and adaptive tool that helps us survive and function in the world. However, beyond managing the ego, individuals can begin to view its reactions—fear, shame, clinging, rage, or excess—as opportunities for self-inquiry. Each challenging emotion carries within it the possibility of its opposite: Darkness can invite humor, clinging can reveal perspective, excess can lead to solitude, and rage can illuminate joy. For example, dark humor often emerges in the very moments when life feels heaviest, and its presence is not accidental; it is a quiet expression of the human capacity to find light within darkness. For example, when people laugh in the midst of grief, trauma, or uncertainty, it is not a denial of pain, but a way of relating to it differently. Levity creates space. It softens the intensity just enough to allow breath, perspective, and even connection with others who understand the experience. In this way, dark humor becomes a form of resilience, an acknowledgment that while suffering is real, it does not have to consume the entirety of our awareness. It reminds us that multiple truths can exist at once: We can be hurting and still find something absurd, ironic, or even beautiful. This capacity to hold both is deeply human. In the midst of darkness, humor does not erase what is difficult, it illuminates our ability to remain alive, aware, and connected, even there. By allowing these emotions and experiences to move through us rather than suppressing them, we begin to recognize that our personality and reactions are not our true identity, but tools that help us learn more about ourselves and our deeper nature.

Helping Professionals

For helping professionals, working with ego structures means moving beyond a focus on fixing symptoms and toward facilitating deeper understanding and integration. Psychotherapy remains essential for stabilizing distress and helping individuals regulate their nervous systems, and within the Labyrinth framework, the ego's responses are also seen as signals that reveal deeper truths about a person's experience. Practitioners can help clients explore what those difficult emotions and reactions are protecting or revealing. This approach encourages curiosity and compassion while allowing clients to fully experience and integrate emotions, rather than resisting them. Approaches such as Internal Family Systems and Dialectical Behavior Therapy already begin to separate ego "parts" from the deeper self and support mindfulness and emotional awareness, and many practitioners are increasingly integrating spiritual or existential perspectives. In this way, therapy becomes not only a process of symptom management or resolution, but also a pathway toward meaning, self-knowledge, and connection with the deeper self.

Institutions and Policy

At the institutional level, this perspective encourages systems to shift from an exclusive emphasis on fixing dysfunction toward supporting understanding, growth, and integration. Symptom relief remains critical, especially when suffering becomes debilitating or life-threatening, but it should not be the only goal of mental health care. When institutions recognize ego structures as part of normal human development, they can design programs that support reflection, emotional processing, creativity, community connection, and meaning-making, alongside clinical interventions. This orientation invites institutions to ask a deeper question when designing care: *Is the goal simply to manage distress, or to support genuine healing and growth?* When meaning and human development are acknowledged as legitimate outcomes of care, individuals are more likely to engage with services in ways that empower them to learn from their experiences and move toward greater participation, resilience, and well-being.

CHAPTER 8:

Inherent Disconnection

Relational Application Critique

The relational application layer encompasses all of our relationships—to our physical selves, our emotional selves, our mental selves, our spiritual selves, our ancestors, our collective community, and our Earth. In our current reality, we tend to primarily focus on our physical and mental selves. When we are in distress, we may then tend to our emotional selves. But what is often dismissed are our spiritual selves, our relationship to our ancestors, our collective, and our Mother Earth. We see these relationships as separate; however, when we really dig in, we can see that in order to be in "right relationship" with one, we need to address all of them. Just as the Labyrinth teaches us, it is all woven together.

The concept of "right relationship" has roots in several philosophical and spiritual traditions, but it is most commonly traced to Indigenous worldviews and Quaker philosophy, where it refers to living in ways that maintain harmony, reciprocity, and ethical responsibility among people, communities, and the natural world. In contemporary leadership and educational contexts, the term has been further articulated by Parker J. Palmer and colleagues, who describe right relationship as the alignment between our inner values, our actions, and our responsibilities to others.[68] Practically, right relationship means engaging with ourselves, others, and the systems we inhabit with integrity, respect, and care. It invites us to cultivate self-awareness, listen deeply, repair harm when it occurs, and act in ways that support mutual flourishing rather than domination or disconnection. In everyday life, practicing right relationship might involve setting healthy boundaries, approaching conflict with curiosity rather than defensiveness, honoring the dignity of others, and making choices that reflect both personal values and collective well-being. Right relationship does not only reference integrity in our relationships with people and things external to us, but also within ourselves.

Right relationship is not just about intentionally acknowledging each part that we need to be in relationship with, but then integrating each part into our day-to-day lives. One may come to understand that their well-being is connected to their body, emotions, community, and environment. Instead of keeping this as an idea, they begin to integrate it into daily life. They notice they've been feeling overwhelmed (emotional self), so rather than pushing through, they take time to pause, breathe, and go for a walk outside (physical + relationship with the Earth). During that walk, they reflect on what they're feeling instead of avoiding it (mental/ emotional awareness). Later, they reach out to a trusted friend to share what's been coming up (community/relational connection). That evening, they take a few quiet moments to sit in stillness or prayer, reconnecting with a deeper sense of meaning or guidance (spiritual self).

In this way, right relationship is not just recognizing that these parts exist, it is actively weaving them into how one lives, responds, and makes decisions each day, allowing life to become more integrated, balanced, and aligned. It is an orientation from which to engage with ourselves and the external world. An analysis of present day trends in right relationship reveals many opportunities for improvement, which will be explored in the forthcoming chapters.

Critique of Present Day Relationships

From Physical

Often we don't pay attention to our bodies until something is wrong. Our bodies must scream at us before we stop to consider what is best for them. We consider aesthetics as a priority over true health. We eat food that is processed, prioritize work over healthy movement, and elect to have major surgeries for cosmetic reasons. Sometimes we don't even take care of our basic food and water needs when we are busy.

From Emotion

It is common to suppress negative emotions in the name of positivity or the desire to appear "put together." We are not in touch with our true emotions because we don't have the proper containers to hold and express them. We fear what fully feeling them might actually do to us.

From Mental

The mental self is the part of us that seeks to understand and respond. It can easily become overwhelmed and cause the emotional self to feel depressed or anxious. Ignoring the mental self looks like not engaging in intellectual stimulation, not seeking knowledge that will aid in moving through life with greater understanding and ease, and not taking the time to understand why we act or respond in the ways we do. This is hard work and, in today's society, many feel that they don't have time or space to truly do the work necessary for their mental self to flourish.

From Spiritual

In the West, there is still a fairly strong and often political divide between religious and non-religious folks. Religion has become polarizing and synonymous with believing in something greater than ourselves. This leaves many people who do not resonate with formal religion without a belief that there is something greater than their minds in their physical bodies, and without a spiritual foundation. When one is without a spiritual foundation, they can become stuck in the first layer, Duality & Fear, as they identify with only their bodies and not their soul. This can lead to a very lopsided engagement with life, which can result in distress, especially when challenging and traumatic life circumstances arrive.

From Ancestors

While many other parts of the world have a strong relationship with their elders and ancestors, the West has developed a culture where the elderly are put in homes and those who have passed are often forgotten. We have lost our connection with elders and their wisdom. We are disconnected from our roots and the fullness of the lives that have come before us and shaped our current realities.

From Collective

With the Industrial Revolution, the West has become individualistic. We have moved into our own homes, with our nuclear families, that need to be supported by each person's individual income. We rely on ourselves for our physical, emotional, and mental well-being. It makes sense that we would then rely on one person (our therapist) to help us when we are struggling. One person cannot do it all. We weren't meant to go through life alone. Policies and systems have been created that reinforce this individualistic way of life.

From the Earth

Mother Earth provides every resource we need to live—water, food, fire, wood, metals, dirt, and air. As we have moved into homes with electricity and running water, have access to food at grocery stores, and have a car to get anywhere we want, we have become disconnected from the Earth. We can go weeks on end without having to truly engage with or touch the Earth with our bare skin. We don't see where our waste goes. We don't directly see the impact we have on air, water, or animals. Because we aren't involved in sourcing materials, we believe there are endless supplies. We can't comprehend the impact we have on Mother Nature because it is largely hidden from us in cities.

Do these present day depictions of our relationship with our physical, emotional, mental, spiritual selves indicate being in right relationship? Does our lack of acknowledgment and connection to our ancestors, community, and the Earth illustrate right relationship?

It is clear that there are many parts of ourselves that we are disconnected from as a product of the society we live in. That doesn't discount that, although we feel disconnected, we can never truly disconnect. We are inherently connected to all parts of ourselves, even if we are blind to it. There is no way around being a part of it all, so it's unavoidable and imperative that we take responsibility and act in right relationship to all of our interconnected parts. This requires awareness and intentionality.

The remainder of the book is dedicated to an exploration of practical applications for how we can reimagine our collective connection and act in right relationship with these seven relationships for the individual, helping professionals, and institutions/organizations.

CHAPTER 9:

Reimagining Relationship to Physical Self

All of life is relational. Relationships are how we learn, love, express, and receive. They are the foundation for life. While all kinds of relationships are opportunities for connection and growth, depth of relationship matters—we will only feel content in our relationships when we are met at the depth we have met ourselves. The deeper we know ourselves, the deeper we can connect with others. The spiral of expansion becomes very clear in this layer of the Labyrinth and is a critical component to accessing the deeper layers of the human experience. Relationships are our mirrors—they are the primary vehicle for knowing ourselves and cultivating a sense of belonging and peace.

We just covered the ways in which we are currently disconnected from all of the various important relationships in our lives. We now turn to identifying how we can repair, strengthen, and flourish in these relationships. We begin with the relationship to our physical self—the self that most of us can easily acknowledge because we can see and touch it.

The nervous system is a big part of our relationship to our bodies—it is what makes us human. Being able to manage and calm the nervous system is the key to accessing the deeper layers of the Labyrinth. It is the system that can unlock deeper layers of connection and awareness. It is the link between our external environment and our ego mind's reaction to it.

The nervous system is the body's communication network, continuously sensing internal and external conditions and coordinating how we respond. It is composed of the central nervous system (the brain and spinal cord), which processes information, and the peripheral nervous system, which carries signals among the brain, body, and environment. Through this system, the body regulates movement, perception, thought, emotion, and vital functions, such as breathing and heart rate. A key part of this network is the autonomic nervous system, which automatically adjusts our state of activation—mobilizing us for action through the sympathetic branch (often associated with fight or flight) or helping us rest, recover, and connect through the parasympathetic branch. In this way, the nervous system acts as a dynamic regulator, constantly balancing safety, threat detection, and restoration to support survival, well-being, and connection. If we want to have access to a resourced nervous system, it's imperative that we are able to connect with our bodies.

Regulation vs. Resourced

We hear the term nervous system regulation thrown around and, while it is important to be able to regulate our reactions to people and events in day-to-day life, it is also important to allow for the full expression of emotions when it's appropriate. If we are trying to stay regulated through a crisis, we are not letting the emotion move through us. This is not being in right relationship with our bodies. Being regulated and resourced are two different things, but they are often conflated. When we are resourced, we are then more likely to stay regulated in day-to-day life. Resourced means priming the body to process big emotions—this can be through breathwork, yoga, exercise, nutrition, etc. It means having an emotional support system with whom to share, and it means a spiritual practice to tether and ground you. We must build the resourcing foundation in our lives in order to be able to fully feel and to be able to return to a regulated state in a reasonable amount of time. It does not make sense, for example, to "stay regulated" when you just received devastating news. That emotion must be felt and have the resourcing to move fully through you without destroying you. When this doesn't happen, it stays in our system and manifests as anxiety, depression, dissociation, freeze response, etc. These manifestations can also happen when you hold in the full expression of an emotion when you are speaking of a past experience and want to avoid "losing it" in therapy, when talking to a friend and don't want to burden them, or when you know you have somewhere to be or something to do. We try to reign it in knowing we don't have the time, space, or support to fully lean in and feel, to crumble. In this way, the emotions stay stuck in the body. We take deep breaths, orient ourselves to the room, etc. to "regulate" ourselves, when we really need a supportive container that gives us enough resourcing to let the emotions be fully felt. Only then can they pass through.

Dissociation is a form of autonomous nervous system regulation. When our bodies are overwhelmed and simply cannot process the magnitude of what we are experiencing, we may automatically go into a dissociated state. Dissociation is a protective mechanism our brains move into when we are not resourced enough to fully feel our current experience. It is a psychological and physiological process in which a person becomes partially disconnected from their thoughts, emotions, body sensations, memories, or surroundings. It is often understood as a protective response of the nervous system that helps the mind cope with overwhelming stress, trauma, or emotional pain by creating distance from an experience that feels too intense to process in the moment. Dissociation can occur on a spectrum, from mild experiences such as spacing out or feeling mentally foggy, to more pronounced disruptions in awareness, memory, or identity. Derealization is a specific form of dissociation in which the external world feels strange, unreal, distant, or dreamlike, even though the person knows intellectually that their surroundings have not changed. People experiencing derealization may describe the world as flat, foggy, or visually distorted, as if they are observing life through a screen or glass. While unsettling, these experiences are generally understood as temporary shifts in perception related to the brain's attempt to regulate overwhelming stress or threat.

We return to the importance of "*and*." Fully feeling emotions is necessary, *and* nervous system resourcing and regulation to manage daily stress is necessary, *and* dissociation is protective, *and* it is not ideal to remain in a dissociated state. The concept of titration is important when we think about working with building capacity in the body and nervous system to be with and fully feel emotions. Titration, in the context of feeling big emotions, refers to the practice of approaching and processing intense emotional experiences in small, manageable doses rather than all at once. Instead of becoming overwhelmed by the full intensity of an emotion, titration involves gently moving in and out of the experience—touching into the feeling, then stepping back to a place of safety or regulation (such as focusing on the breath, the body, or the present environment). This allows the nervous system to gradually build the capacity to tolerate and process the emotion without shutting down or becoming flooded. In essence, titration is about pacing emotional processing, so that healing can occur in a way that is sustainable, embodied, and supportive rather than overwhelming.

We can build capacity through somatic work (many options for this are listed at this end of this chapter). Once we have increased capacity, in a supported environment, we can dip our toe into the thing we have been too overwhelmed to feel. We feel to our limit, allowing the emotion to move through our physical bodies as much as we can tolerate. When we feel the overwhelm happening again, we can come back to our bodies and return to the somatic work of capacity-building and expansion. This is done over and over, little by little. Slowly building capacity—opening, feeling, and returning to safety. This relationship to the physical body can't be rushed.

When alchemizing pain, the body must stabilize before diving deep into the emotional territory. If we try to dive deep into a physical system that is contracted or in a state of overwhelm, the person can enter a state of freeze, panic or psychosis.

Tending to & Listening to Our Bodies

Sometimes, we need to begin with the basics. Nutrition, temperature regulation, sleep, hydration, sunlight, and movement are foundational and are required before our bodies and nervous systems even have a chance to expand and strengthen. We are more similar to plants than we realize. We must tend to these basic needs before any nervous system capacity-building or deep emotional processing can be truly lasting and effective.

When awareness is moved from the head/mind into the body, we enter into a state of noticing sensations over stories. Our ego mind can make up many stories, often created from fear. Moving awareness into the body allows for communication to happen in a direct way, without the story. This is what some might call tapping into your inner knowing, inner wisdom, or intuition. Listening to the body allows the sensations that are felt to inform our minds of what we are truly feeling without the mind taking over. The physical discomfort from emotions is our teacher—it tells us that something is not right. When we get to a point where we are so uncomfortable in the body, we must listen. This is often where dis-ease or severe anxiety enter the picture. We can no longer ignore what the body is telling us. The opposite is also true—when the body feels lightness and ease, it is communicating that we are on the right path and that our actions are in alignment with our emotions. Although the body's communication can result in discomfort or illness, this isn't a bad thing. It is the body's way of getting our attention when we have been trying to dissociate or ignore what is going on emotionally. This tension is necessary for acknowledgment and subsequent growth and transformation. Physical discomfort is one of our greatest motivators and teachers. We must learn to listen sooner, rather than later. Our bodies will continually ramp up the dis-ease and dis-comfort until we do.

Moving Stuck Energy

Creating a physical environment where the nervous system is resourced and mostly regulated is a bit of the chicken or the egg dilemma. While we need to build capacity to feel, that capacity will not be sufficient if stuck energies haven't been moved and processed. It's a delicate dance to move energy and build capacity at the same time. The trick is to find a modality that allows access to and movement of energies in a way that doesn't overwhelm the system as it's being built. The intention isn't to create a container that can hold it all—it is to create a container that is resourced to fully feel an emotion in order to let it pass through. When it doesn't pass through, a backlog is created, and no amount of capacity-building can alleviate the symptoms that come from the accumulation of these unprocessed experiences. There are specific practices that are meant to help move and process heavy energies—Conscious Connected Breathwork, Somatic Experiencing, Tension and Trauma Releasing Exercises (TRE), energy work, and plant medicine are highly effective. Some practices are more gentle than others, and it's important to find the right fit to match the level of resourcing your nervous system is currently experiencing.

Physical Connection Practices

How do we engage in reconnecting with our physical bodies? There are many somatic practices available—some are led by those with formal training, and others you can learn and do on your own or in community.

On Your Own/In Community

- Crying
- Tantric Yoga
- Kundalini Yoga
- Energy center work (Chakras)
- Dance/Ecstatic dance

- Conscious Connected Breathwork/Kriya Yoga
- Pranayama
- Bhakti yoga
- Singing
- Listening to or creating music
- Tapping
- Qi Gong
- Tai Chi
- Aromatherapy
- Exercise
- Yoga
- Sound baths
- Nurturing touch
- Trauma Releasing Exercises

Require Training

- Craniosacral/energy work
- Massage
- Yomassage
- Chiropractic
- Acupuncture
- Somatic processing with the use of transpersonal medicine

Practical Applications of Cultivating a Relationship with the Physical Self

Individuals

For individuals, developing a healthy relationship with the physical self begins with honoring the body as a central source of information, regulation, and wisdom. This starts with being intentional about the foundations of physical care: adequate sleep, nourishing food, movement, hydration, and rest, while recognizing that these basic practices form the groundwork for overall well-being. Beyond foundational care, individuals can deepen their relationship with the body by incorporating somatic practices into daily life. These may include yoga, stretching, breathwork, mindful walking, body scans, dance, or other forms of conscious movement that encourage awareness of bodily sensations. Somatic practices help individuals reconnect with the body's natural rhythms and signals, strengthening interoception, the ability to sense what is happening internally. As this awareness develops, people can begin to trust the body's intelligence rather than relying solely on the thinking mind, which can sometimes override or dismiss physical cues. By regularly pausing to check in with the body, asking what it needs, noticing tension or ease, and allowing movement or rest when necessary, individuals cultivate a more balanced relationship between body, mind, and emotion.

Helping Professionals

Helping professionals can support this relationship by encouraging clients to reconnect with their bodies as an important component of healing and self-understanding. Many individuals are accustomed to processing experiences primarily through thoughts and narratives, yet the body often carries valuable information about stress, safety, and emotional experience. Practitioners can gently guide clients to notice physical sensations during sessions, such as changes in breath, posture, or muscle tension, and explore what these sensations may be communicating. Incorporating brief somatic practices, grounding exercises, or mindful movement within sessions can help clients build comfort with body awareness. Professionals can also provide resources, referrals, or recommendations for practices such as yoga, body-based therapies, breathwork, or movement programs that support somatic awareness outside of sessions. By emphasizing the importance of the body in processing experiences and regulating emotions, helping professionals help clients develop a more integrated relationship with themselves.

Institutions and Policy

At the institutional and policy level, supporting the physical self means recognizing that physical care and embodied awareness are essential components of overall wellness. Schools, workplaces, and community organizations can prioritize environments that encourage movement, rest, and body awareness throughout the day. This may include providing opportunities for physical activity, creating spaces for stretching or mindful breaks, and integrating somatic practices into wellness programming. Community initiatives might offer accessible classes in yoga, movement, breathwork, or other body-based practices that help individuals reconnect with their physical selves. Institutions can also promote policies that support healthy work-life balance, regular breaks, and environments designed to reduce chronic stress on the body. By emphasizing the importance of caring for and listening to the body, institutions help create cultures where physical well-being is recognized as a foundation for mental, emotional, and social health.

CHAPTER 10:

Reimagining Relationship to Spirit Self

"The salvation of man is through love and in love. I understood how a man who has nothing left in this world still may know bliss, be it only for a brief moment, in the contemplation of his beloved. In a position of utter desolation, when man cannot express himself in positive action, when his only achievement may consist in enduring his sufferings in the right way—an honourable way— in such a position man can, through loving contemplation of the image he carries of his beloved, achieve fulfilment." —Viktor Frankl, *Man's Search for Meaning*

It is easy to get caught up in our material world, thinking that the only things that are real, can be seen. It takes intentionality and stillness to remember that we are more than our physical bodies. When we forget that we are more than our bodies, we can feel less than whole. Perhaps we feel a void, emptiness, or a lack of meaning. Returning to the wholeness of our soul occupying the human body allows us to feel a greater sense of peace. When we are able to connect with ourselves on a soul level, we understand that we are love and light at our essence. We experience the depths of all emotions—those we deem good and bad—so that we can truly know ourselves. How can we know pure love without experiencing hate? How can we know light without dark? How can we know ease without heaviness?

Knowing and working with our spirit selves is termed transpersonal. Transpersonal work refers to approaches to healing and personal development that include, but also move beyond, the individual ego and mind to explore deeper dimensions of human experience such as meaning, purpose, interconnectedness, and spiritual awareness. Transpersonal work allows the ego (the default mode network in the brain) to be set aside during the experience and softened afterward to allow for exploration of the innermost layers of the Labyrinth that are often elusive to humans with their ego mind fully online. The Default Mode Network (DMN) is a network in the brain that becomes active when we are not focused on the outside world—when the mind is at rest, wandering, reflecting, remembering, or imagining. It is closely associated with self-referential thinking, meaning the way we think about ourselves: our identity, our past, our future, and how we fit into the world. Because of this, the DMN is often considered the neural correlate of what many traditions call the "ego."[69]

In practical terms, the DMN is what generates the ongoing inner narrative: *Who am I? What happened to me? What will happen next? What do others think of me?* It helps organize our sense of self over time, which is essential for functioning in daily life. In this way, the DMN—and the ego—are not problems; they are necessary tools for identity, planning, and social navigation.

However, when the DMN becomes overactive or rigid, it can reinforce repetitive patterns such as rumination, worry, and self-criticism. This is where the connection to ego becomes more apparent: The mind gets caught in loops of protective stories, fears, and identity structures that feel absolute rather than flexible. For example, someone might repeatedly think, *"I'm not good enough,"* or *"This always happens to me,"* which reflects the ego trying to create stability, but is instead limiting perspective.

Practices that reduce DMN dominance—such as mindfulness, meditation, breathwork, somatic awareness, certain therapeutic approaches and plant medicine—often lead to a loosening of ego identification. People may report feeling less caught in their thoughts, more present in their bodies, and more connected to others or to a broader sense of self. Neuroscientifically, this corresponds to decreased activity in the DMN and increased activity in networks related to present-moment awareness. The goal is not to eliminate the DMN or the ego, but to develop a flexible relationship with it—to be able to use it when needed, while also stepping outside of it to access deeper awareness, presence, and meaning.

Emerging from the field of transpersonal psychology in the late 1960s, associated with thinkers such as Abraham Maslow, Stanislav Grof, and Anthony Sutich, and influenced by earlier pioneers like Carl Jung, this perspective recognizes that psychological growth can involve transformative states of consciousness, expanded identity, and experiences of connection with something larger than oneself. Rather than focusing only on symptom reduction, transpersonal approaches aim to support wholeness, helping people reconnect with their inner resources, values, and sense of belonging within the larger web of life.

You can see that this connection to spirit self is highly correlated with connection to physical self. When we begin to see that there is truly no separation of body and spirit, we know that a connection with our physical bodies is the same as a connection to our spirit self. To fully connect with our spirit self, we must go deep within our bodies. This connection is not outside of ourselves, but deep within. As stated in the Emerald Tablet (a widely influential ancient text in Europe during the Middle Ages and Renaissance, with influential translations made by figures such as Isaac Newton), "As above, so below," meaning the macrocosm (universe) and microcosm (human form/soul) reflect each other.[70] Transpersonal approaches help us to understand that the separation is a false reality we have constructed. One way we can feel this connection between our physical self and our spirit self is by noticing our consciousness. Usually when we are still and intentionally take the time to notice our awareness, we find it in the head/mind. By allowing yourself to notice it in the head and consciously move it into the body/heart space, you will find that once fully in the body, you can just be/exist without question. You may feel ease, love, joy, and contentment.

Understanding that we are more than just physical bodies plays a large role in moving through grief. The thought that we cease to exist after our death creates an unnecessary component to grief. When we can connect with ourselves beyond our bodies, we have internal proof that we are more than our material form. When we have that strong inner knowing, connecting with loved ones regardless of their physical form becomes possible. Changing the narrative around what physical death truly means takes an enormous burden off of the person grieving. It does not eliminate grief, but it certainly makes it more manageable, and it can bring acceptance within reach.

The following practices may help cultivate transpersonal awareness and experience:

- Meditation
- Prayer
- Drumming
- Storytelling
- Dreamwork
- Lucid dreaming
- Child-like playfulness/expressions of joy
- Creativity in any form
- Therapeutic, guided and integrated plant medicine/transpersonal journeys
- Experiences with After Death Communication (ADC)
- Exploring Sacred Geometry in our physical environment (The Fibonacci Spiral, The Flower of Life, The Circle, etc.)
- Time spent in nature
- Consciousness studies (studying the science behind quantum physics, near-death experiences, mediumship, reincarnation)
- Yoga for Living by Yomassage
- Awe-inspiring experiences (often in nature)

Practical Applications of Cultivating a Relationship with the Spiritual Self

Individuals

For individuals, developing a relationship with the spiritual self begins with creating intentional space to explore who you are beyond the physical body and the thinking mind. While the body and brain are central to human experience, many people also experience a deeper sense of identity, connected to meaning, purpose, awareness, or what some traditions describe as the soul or spirit. Exploring this dimension may involve reflective practices such as meditation, prayer, contemplative journaling, time in nature, creative expression, or quiet self-inquiry. Questions like, *What gives my life meaning?* or *What feels deeply true or aligned within me?* can help individuals connect with this deeper layer of self. Engaging with spirituality does not require adherence to a specific religion; rather, it often involves cultivating a sense of connection to oneself, to others, to nature, or to something larger than the individual self. Through these practices, individuals may develop a greater sense of peace, perspective, and purpose, helping them navigate life's challenges with a deeper understanding of their place in the world.

Helping Professionals

Helping professionals can support clients in exploring the spiritual dimension of their experience by creating safe and respectful spaces where conversations about meaning, purpose, and deeper identity are welcomed. This may involve gently guiding clients beyond the narratives of the mind or the immediate sensations of the body to explore questions such as, *Who is observing these thoughts and sensations?* or *What part of you remains steady even when experiences change?* Encouraging clients to reflect on their sense of self beyond roles, identities, or past experiences can open pathways to deeper awareness. Professionals may also introduce or support practices that help clients connect with this dimension of self such as mindfulness, contemplative practices, creative expression, or nature-based reflection while remaining respectful of each client's personal beliefs and cultural background. In doing so, practitioners help clients explore a sense of inner presence or essence that can provide grounding, perspective, and meaning, particularly during times of uncertainty or transition.

Institutions and Policy

At the institutional and policy level, supporting the spiritual dimension of well-being involves recognizing that human health includes questions of meaning, belonging, and connection to something larger than oneself. Institutions such as schools, workplaces, and healthcare systems can create environments where discussions about purpose, values, and personal meaning are normalized and respected. This may include offering spaces for reflection, quiet contemplation, spiritual support, or nature-based activities that allow individuals to reconnect with deeper aspects of themselves. Recognizing the importance of soul or spirit expression through creativity, play, joy, community connection, and engagement with the natural world can also support holistic well-being. Institutions can acknowledge that, for many people, spiritual frameworks help them make sense of life transitions, suffering, and grief, including experiences surrounding loss and death. By recognizing the role that spiritual connection can play in helping individuals feel at ease in their bodies, find meaning in their lives, and process profound life experiences, institutions help foster cultures that honor the full depth of human experience.

CHAPTER 11:

Reimagining the Relationship to Mental Self

The relationship we have with our mental self was largely covered in our exploration of ego management through therapy. As much as we might feel like our mind can act as the enemy, it's important to understand that it is, in fact, a very real part of the human experience, and cultivating a healthy relationship with the mind is imperative to be able to fully engage with all of the other relationships with ourselves. The mind is powerful and, if we let it, it's possible for it to take over the fullness of our human experience. It's important to keep the mind "in check" and to use it to its fullest potential. Similar to how the Human Experience Labyrinth orients us to the path we walk through life, this can only be done when we are aware of the mind's role in life. It exists for a reason.

Service

One of the most effective ways to quiet the story of our mental selves, is to be of service to others. When we get out of our own heads and stories about our own suffering and begin noticing those around us, the stories begin to disappear. Our focus shifts to alleviating suffering for others, witnessing, being present with, and attuning to something outside of ourselves. This shift in focus allows for an exploration into what feels meaningful and in alignment with who we are—what gifts do we possess that can be used to help others? How have our own sufferings prepared us to be of service to others?

Once again, we return to the importance of purpose, meaning, and alignment and how all of these parts intersect and influence each other. The mental self has to understand and be in alignment with what its purpose is in life, which is often communicated by our spirit selves. We can know when our mental self and our spirit self are not being heard by tuning into our physical self— when we are ignoring something important, our bodies will always allow us to feel the physical sensation of unease. To determine meaning and purpose, one must cultivate the relationship and connection with all parts of self.

Ram Dass says that to be an "impeccable human" we must let our "being" (our true self, love) shine through into our "doing."[71] We were born with specific personality traits and gifts that are unique to us. While these are technically part of the ego, we can use them for good. For example, I am a compulsive thinker. I analyze, decipher, dig, research, experiment, process, and then I want to share via writing, speaking, and teaching. These skills and traits come from my mind and personality. I can choose to use them for good—letting them be guided by love and shine through that lens into my "doing." Or, they can compulsively take over and limit my access to the other parts of my being. When we keep the mind "in check," we are well-rounded and strategically utilizing each part of ourselves for the best outcome ... fully embodied, meaningful, creative expression and contribution, and growth.

On a personal level, this leads to a feeling of internal power, alignment, calm, and contentment. On a societal level, when an individual is able to use their ego powers in service of their larger contribution to the world, everyone benefits. To function optimally, the mind must be limited to its functional role and then integrated with the spirit.

There are many approaches that have been developed to tame and train the mind. Effective approaches for developing a healthy relationship with the mind include:

- Therapy/psychoanalysis
- Volunteering/being of service
- Interpersonal skills building
- Internal nervous system skills building
- Psycho-Education (understanding of self, philosophy)

- Giving up the need to understand/surrender
- "Soul work" concepts to manage ego: gratitude, perspective, acceptance, surrender, control, etc.

Practical Applications of Cultivating a Relationship with the Mental Self

Individuals

For individuals, cultivating a healthy relationship with the mental self begins with recognizing that the mind is a powerful tool, but it is not the entirety of who we are. Thoughts, beliefs, and mental narratives shape how we interpret the world, yet they are only one aspect of the broader human experience. Developing awareness of the mind allows individuals to observe thoughts rather than becoming completely identified with them. Practices such as meditation, reflective journaling, cognitive reframing, and mindfulness can help individuals notice patterns of thinking and gently redirect the mind when it becomes caught in worry, rumination, or self-criticism. When the mind is approached with curiosity rather than judgment, individuals can begin to use it intentionally to analyze, problem-solve, and create, while remaining grounded in their emotional, physical, and relational experiences. In this way, the mind becomes a supportive partner rather than the sole driver of one's life. Volunteering or being of service is a practical way to give the mind a break and identify what ignites a feeling of passion and purpose.

Helping Professionals

Helping professionals play an important role in helping clients understand that many therapeutic interventions are designed to help regulate and organize the mind, particularly when thoughts become overwhelming or distorted. Cognitive and behavioral approaches, for example, provide valuable tools for identifying patterns, challenging unhelpful beliefs, and building healthier mental habits. At the same time, professionals can help clients recognize that true integration often requires engaging with other aspects of the self, beyond the cognitive realm. Encouraging clients to build relationships with their emotional experiences, bodily sensations, intuition, and social environments can create a more complete sense of self-understanding. Encouraging clients to be of service provides a tangible opportunity to get out of one's head and move toward meaning making. By framing mental tools as one component within a larger ecosystem of human experience, helping professionals can support clients in developing both clarity of thought and deeper personal awareness.

Institutions and Policy

At the institutional and policy level, supporting the mental self involves providing individuals with tools that help them manage stress, attention, and cognitive demands while also acknowledging that human well-being extends beyond mental productivity and physical health alone. Schools, workplaces, and healthcare systems can incorporate programs that teach skills such as mindfulness, emotional regulation, and reflective thinking, helping individuals build healthier relationships with their minds. At the same time, institutions can broaden their language and frameworks around wellness to include emotional, relational, and experiential dimensions of health. By normalizing conversations about mental awareness alongside other aspects of human experience, institutions help create cultures that value balance, reflection, and whole-person development rather than focusing solely on cognitive performance or efficiency. All systems would benefit from encouraging and providing opportunities to be of service.

CHAPTER 12:

Reimagining Relationship to Emotional Self

We can talk until the cows come home, but reliving the same story and associated emotions from past experiences can not only reinforce our identification with those experiences and emotions, but it also can keep us from moving the felt experience through our bodies. While understanding what happened and identifying emotions is part of the healing puzzle, we often end there. The missing steps are to feel those emotions in our bodies, and then do the work to help those sensations move through and out.

Often, we stuff our emotions. We resist fully feeling them for fear that they will consume us or we won't be able to handle the intensity. Maybe we want to go with the flow and not cause disruption to a relationship or our lives, so we pretend that we are fine. We can easily become disconnected from our emotions. Unfortunately, ignoring emotions doesn't make them not exist. It just stores them in our body until our systems are at capacity, and then we involuntarily explode or express it as dis-ease or anxiety in the body.

In the discussion on reimagining the relationship to our physical self, building capacity in the body was highlighted. This is an integral part of being able to fully connect with the emotional self. Being witnessed, held, and offered co-regulation by someone being present with you as you experience the depths of your emotions is a powerful and necessary component to feeling safe enough to fully feel. It is also helpful to understand that, by the simple act of observing your emotions, you notice that you are not, in fact, your emotions. You are the consciousness observing your physical body feeling the emotion. Once we can create distance between ourselves and the emotion, it is perceived as safer to allow the emotions to exist.

Research shows that if allowed to be felt and moved, our emotions only last sixty to ninety seconds. The suffering that comes with emotions lies in the mind creating stories or replaying the event that caused the emotion. If we can be intentional about moving awareness from the mind to the body (as described in the previous chapter), and then allow for the full feeling of an emotion to be felt and then dissipate, we can live in more presence and ease. The resistance to feeling emotions is what causes the congestion that builds in the body and impacts the nervous system. Emotions are like the weather, and the body is like the sky. The weather must have space to pass through. If the storm is not allowed to pass through, it will build and build, creating a back up from new storms that have been created and stifled. Life doesn't stop creating experiences that elicit emotion, just like the storms don't disappear because we desire a sunny day instead of a storm.

What is the baseline of our true "self" underneath the emotions? What qualities does the sky have? It has the capacity to hold the storm. It is consistent, present, and allows for flow. It holds both the storms and the sunny days, the light and the dark. The standard state of our true selves reflects that of the sky. Once we let the emotional storm pass through, we can return to our baseline state of ease.

Creating time and space to feel—while recognizing that we are not our emotions and that the mind does not need to replay every story, allows us to move through life with greater ease. This illustrates the concept of presence—living in the now. It is not easy, but with knowledge and intention, it is possible to return to presence when we have been pulled into suffering.

Below are some helpful approaches for connecting with the emotional self:

- Journal
- Create space from and observe the mental self

- Create time and space to feel emotions in the physical body
- Move the physical body to allow emotions to also move through the body (exercise, dance, breathing, etc)
- Limit replaying stories
- Understand that we must feel the full range of emotions (challenging and joyful) if we want to truly know ourselves. We can't know the full expression of joy without the full expression of despair
- Zoom Out. Spend time with the visual meditation of emotions as the storm and the baseline state as the sky
- Adjust your language. Name what is being felt without identifying with it. Ex:. I am feeling anxious right now vs. I am anxious
- Identify a safe person to be present with you as you feel your emotions (attuned friend, guide, therapist, somatic facilitator, etc.)

Practical Application

Individuals

For individuals, developing a healthy relationship with the emotional self begins with building the capacity to feel emotions within the body rather than becoming overwhelmed or defined by them. Emotions are natural physiological responses that arise, move through the body, and eventually resolve when given space and attention. Practically, this means learning to notice where emotions show up physically, such as tightness in the chest, warmth in the face, heaviness in the stomach, or tension in the shoulders, and allowing those sensations to be experienced without immediately reacting to them. Individuals can practice disidentifying from emotions, recognizing that emotions are temporary experiences rather than fixed identities. Creating intentional time and space to feel through practices such as breathwork, body scans, movement, or quiet reflection can help people process emotions in a healthy way. It is also important to notice when the mind is bypassing or resisting emotional experience, such as through distraction, intellectualization, or avoidance. By gently bringing attention back to the body and allowing feelings to move through, individuals can build resilience and emotional regulation while maintaining a deeper sense of inner stability and self-compassion. It is important to identify someone who can sit beside you and offer support while deeply accessing your emotions.

Helping Professionals

Helping professionals can support clients in developing this relationship by helping them understand that they are not their emotions, but rather observers and experiencers of them. While sharing personal stories can be helpful in the initial stages of processing, repeatedly retelling narratives may sometimes reinforce emotional loops rather than facilitating integration. Instead, professionals can guide clients toward approaches that emphasize embodied emotional processing, helping them notice how emotions manifest physically and allowing those sensations to move through the body. Somatic practices such as grounding exercises, breath regulation, mindful movement, or body awareness techniques can help clients increase their tolerance for emotional experiences without becoming overwhelmed. Practitioners can also help clients identify patterns of emotional avoidance, or bypassing, and gently support them in building the capacity to stay present with their feelings. By combining compassionate presence with body-based awareness, helping professionals can guide clients toward experiencing emotions as dynamic processes that arise, move, and resolve, rather than fixed states that define them.

Institutions and Policy

At the institutional and policy level, recognizing the importance of emotional processing means acknowledging that emotions are not only psychological experiences but also physiological ones that require space and regulation. Schools, workplaces, and community organizations can integrate somatic and emotional awareness practices into wellness programs, recognizing that individuals often carry emotional responses to stress, conflict, or major life events within their bodies. Institutions can normalize practices that support emotional regulation, such as mindfulness breaks, movement opportunities, quiet reflection spaces, and trauma-informed programming. Training staff and leaders in basic emotional and somatic awareness can also help create environments where emotional experiences are acknowledged without stigma. Policies that support time for reflection, rest, and stress recovery can further reinforce the understanding that emotional well-being is a core component of overall health. By intentionally creating environments that allow people to process and move emotions through the body, institutions help foster cultures of resilience, self-awareness, and collective well-being.

CHAPTER 13:

Reimagining Relationship to Community

Reconnecting with the collective is a remembering. This is where we came from. The advent of the Industrial Revolution has taken us far away from our communities, and with each problem that arises as a product of this isolation, we create a new "formal" intervention to address it. It's time we stop building the independent scaffolding in society that is clearly not working, and reorient to focus on finding wisdom, witnessing each other, and cultivating deep connection within our communities. This is already happening on a grassroots level in parts of the West. There are micro-communities found all over who have felt this deeply and are creating their own versions of collectivist living or mutual aid.

Applying the concept of right relationship to the collective reveals how much modern life has drifted toward isolation. In many communities today, people live side-by-side yet remain largely unknown to one another, sometimes unaware even of a neighbor's name, let alone their struggles. Right relationship asks something deeper of us. It calls us to recognize that our lives are interconnected and that understanding and supporting one another is part of living well, together. But connection alone is not enough; true community grows through resonance. Resonance emerges when people meet not only in shared experience but in shared orientation—similar intentions, values, and ways of approaching life's challenges. Consider a support group where every participant has endured the same event but holds a different relationship to it: One person remains stuck in *"why me?"* while another seeks to understand *why does this happen to anyone?*, while another searches for the meaning it may hold within their life story, *what is my personal why?*. Though they share an experience, their internal frameworks shape whether they can truly resonate with one another. Resonance is what allows communities to move beyond proximity and into genuine connection, where understanding deepens, support becomes natural, and individuals feel held within a shared way of making sense of life.

The Human Experience Labyrinth offers a framework that can help restore this sense of resonance within communities. When individuals begin to understand that human life moves through recognizable layers—suffering and fear, ego responses, relational experience, embodied awareness, and eventually integration and meaning—they gain a shared language for navigating hardship. Instead of interpreting challenges through entirely different paradigms, people can begin to recognize where they and others might be within the Labyrinth. Someone may still be in the outer rings, grappling with fear or identity disruption, while another may have moved toward reflection and meaning-making. Rather than judging or misunderstanding one another, the Labyrinth allows community members to see these differences as different places along the same path. This shared orientation creates the conditions for resonance: Individuals can meet one another with empathy, knowing that each stage is part of the human journey. In this way, the Labyrinth does not eliminate differences in experience, but it provides a common map that allows people to recognize themselves and each other within the same unfolding process, making deeper connection and mutual support possible.

Witnessing

Being seen, understood, and witnessed is an essential component to this human experience. Having your experience mirrored back through witnessing is crucial. Imagine suffering in isolation, having no one acknowledge the depth of your hurt. Human beings are fundamentally social, and sustained isolation from community can have profound psychological, emotional, and physical consequences. When people lack meaningful connection and belonging, the nervous system often interprets this absence as a form of threat, which can increase stress, anxiety, and feelings of depression. Social isolation has been associated with higher rates of loneliness, substance use, and suicidal ideation, as well as physical health risks such as weakened immune function, sleep disruption, and cardiovascular problems. Beyond individual symptoms, isolation can erode a person's sense of identity, purpose, and hope, since many aspects of meaning and resilience are shaped through relationships and shared experiences. Community provides feedback, care, and a sense of being seen; without it, individuals may struggle to regulate emotions, maintain perspective during hardship, and feel connected to something larger than themselves.

Respect, Responsibility, Rights & Reciprocity

Healthy communities are sustained by shared values that guide how people relate to one another, including respect, responsibility, rights, and reciprocity.

Respect involves recognizing the inherent dignity and worth of each person, listening to different perspectives, and honoring the diversity of experiences and identities within a group. We must also respect sovereignty and a person's control over their own decisions and existence.

Responsibility reflects the understanding that each member has a role in caring for the well-being of the whole, contributing their efforts, and acting in ways that support collective trust and safety. We must recognize that we have a responsibility to ourselves (which then serves as the ripple effect into our communities) and altruistically helping others without attachment to outcomes. We must be willing to offer our presence, tools, and compassion whether or not the recipient is grateful, utilizes it, or improves from it.

Rights ensure that individuals are protected and able to participate fully in community life, with their voices, needs, and boundaries acknowledged and upheld. Each person should have the same rights, regardless of their place in society.

Reciprocity weaves these values together by emphasizing mutual care—an ongoing exchange in which people both give and receive support, knowledge, and resources. When these principles are practiced together, they create the conditions for communities where individuals feel valued, accountable to one another, and connected through shared commitment and care.

Vulnerability & Authenticity

In order for communities to lean into witnessing, sharing, and unconditional reciprocity, individuals must be able to access their vulnerability. They have to "be real" about their struggles and also feel confident in what they can offer to the community. Our current society gives us points for being strong, working hard, figuring things out on our own, and "succeeding." It can feel as if we are a failure if we let our needs be known or if we seem "imperfect." We must embrace and honor the collective struggle. One way we can cultivate that in our community is to serve as an example. Be the one who shares a real personal struggle. Be honest about the highs and lows of life. Ask for help. Take the masks off that we unconsciously put on in order to not "rock the boat." Be authentic.

Have you ever heard of the Benjamin Franklin effect? The Benjamin Franklin effect refers to the psychological phenomenon in which a person who does a favor for someone is more likely to feel positively toward that person afterward. The term comes from an observation by Benjamin Franklin, who wrote that asking a rival to lend him a book helped transform the relationship into a friendlier one.[72] Psychologists explain this effect through cognitive dissonance: When we help someone, our minds tend to conclude that we must value or like that person, because our actions suggest they are worth helping. As a result, acts of giving can actually strengthen feelings of connection and goodwill toward the recipient. In the context of altruism, this effect highlights how helping behaviors can reinforce prosocial attitudes and relationships within communities. When individuals contribute time, care, or resources to others, those actions can deepen empathy, strengthen social bonds, and encourage ongoing cycles of generosity and cooperation. This is the kind of iterative cycle that strengthens communities.

The Tide is Turning

There is a noticeable shift in parts of Western societies toward more communal, interdependent ways of living. While uneven, and often driven by economic pressures as much as ideology, this shift is visible across a range of tangible practices:

- Mutual aid networks have expanded significantly, particularly since the COVID-19 pandemic. These are grassroots systems where individuals directly support one another with resources such as food, housing assistance, childcare, and transportation. Unlike traditional charity models, mutual aid operates horizontally, emphasizing reciprocity and shared responsibility rather than top-down giving.
- Co-housing and intentional communities are growing in both urban and rural settings. These models combine private living spaces with shared resources such as kitchens, gardens, and childcare. Rising housing costs and increasing social isolation are major drivers behind this trend.
- Community fridges and free stores have become more common in many cities. These publicly accessible resources operate on a "take what you need, leave what you can" principle, addressing food insecurity through collective contribution and access.
- Cooperative business models, including worker-owned cooperatives and food co-ops, are gaining traction as alternatives to traditional corporate structures. These models distribute ownership, decision-making, and profits more equitably among participants.

- Tool libraries and resource-sharing initiatives allow communities to share access to equipment, tools, and other goods. Often paired with repair cafés, these efforts reduce individual ownership burdens while fostering collaboration and sustainability.
- Collective childcare and parenting networks have re-emerged in various forms, including informal childcare exchanges, homeschooling cooperatives, and learning pods. These arrangements reduce costs while strengthening social bonds among families.
- Community-supported agriculture (CSA) programs connect individuals directly with local farms. Participants purchase shares of a farm's output, reinforcing local food systems and creating mutual reliance between producers and consumers.
- Community-based health and care collectives provide support, such as transportation to medical appointments, elder care, and mental health assistance. These networks often emerge where formal healthcare systems are inaccessible or insufficient.
- Time banking and alternative economic systems enable people to exchange services based on time rather than money. Local currencies and barter networks similarly reflect efforts to revalue labor and reduce dependence on traditional financial systems.
- Tiny home villages and cooperative housing models for unhoused populations emphasize shared governance and community responsibility. These approaches contrast with more impersonal shelter systems by prioritizing stability and social connection.
- Digital platforms have facilitated new forms of community organizing. Online tools enable rapid coordination of mutual aid, crowdfunding for emergencies, and the formation of localized support networks.
- Skill-sharing initiatives and commons-based learning environments promote the idea that knowledge should

be collectively owned and freely exchanged. These often take place through workshops, maker spaces, and community-led education.

- Restorative and community justice practices offer alternatives to punitive legal systems. These approaches focus on repairing harm through dialogue, accountability, and reintegration rather than punishment.
- Shared mobility systems, including bike-sharing and car-sharing programs, reduce the need for individual ownership and reflect a broader shift toward collective infrastructure use.

In addition to the list above, some simple approaches to cultivate community include the following:

- Grief ceremony/sharing circles.
- Somatic practices like Tai Chi, breathwork, yoga, dancing, etc., in community settings.
- Informal restorative justice circles vs. shunning. This creates opportunities for repair, deepening trust and strengthening relationships.
- Focus on forgiveness. When we can forgive others, that often means we can forgive ourselves, too. More grace for all leads to more internal and external peace—within ourselves and in our communities.

Practical Applications of Cultivating a Relationship with Community

Individuals

For individuals, cultivating a relationship with community begins with recognizing that human beings are inherently relational. We were not meant to move through life in isolation; our well-being is deeply shaped by the presence, support, and shared experiences of others. Community offers spaces where people can feel seen, understood, and supported through both challenges and celebrations. Practically, this means making intentional efforts to build and nurture relationships—checking in on neighbors, participating in local gatherings, volunteering, joining groups with shared interests, or simply spending meaningful time with others. An important part of this process is the willingness to practice vulnerability, allowing others to see our authentic experiences rather than presenting a polished or guarded version of ourselves. When individuals lean into openness, mutual support, and shared responsibility, communities become places where belonging and resilience can grow. It's important to offer this, even if you don't feel like you are receiving it from your community. This cycle has to start somewhere and it might as well be with you!

Helping Professionals

Helping professionals can support community connection by recognizing that individual work alone is often insufficient for sustained healing and growth. While one-on-one support can be valuable, many of the struggles people face such as loneliness, shame, and disconnection are best addressed within relational and communal contexts. Professionals can encourage clients to engage in group therapy, peer support groups, community circles, or shared activities that foster connection with others experiencing similar challenges. They can also help clients identify safe and supportive spaces in their own neighborhoods or networks where relationships can develop naturally. Importantly, helping professionals benefit from modeling these principles themselves by cultivating community in their own lives—participating in neighborhood activities, engaging in peer consultation groups, and building professional networks that emphasize collaboration rather than isolation. When practitioners value and practice community in their own lives, they reinforce the idea that healing and well-being often happen within collective relationships rather than solely through individual effort.

Institutions and Policy

At the institutional and policy level, fostering healthy communities requires a commitment to collective care and relational culture. Organizations, schools, and workplaces can serve as powerful examples by prioritizing environments where people feel valued, supported, and connected. This includes taking care of employees and students as whole people, recognizing that their mental, emotional, physical, and spiritual well-being all contribute to their ability to thrive. Institutions can integrate community-building practices into daily routines, such as shared check-ins, collaborative problem-solving, mentorship structures, and opportunities for meaningful dialogue. Approaches like restorative justice can replace punitive systems with processes that focus on accountability, repair, and relationship-building. Policies that encourage collaboration, transparency, and mutual support help create cultures where vulnerability is not seen as weakness but as a foundation for trust. When institutions actively model community care and collective responsibility, they help normalize the understanding that well-being is not only an individual pursuit but a shared and communal endeavor.

CHAPTER 14:

Reimagining Relationship to Ancestors

While living in the present moment is important, we are missing out on wisdom that can aid us in moving through this life when we don't engage with our elders and ancestors. In today's society, not only do we not engage with our elders or ancestors, but we actively discount the elderly, giving much more credence and weight to what those who are young and "successful" have to contribute. There is no reason to recreate the wheel and figure life out all on our own—we have elders and ancestors for a reason. There is much to learn from how our ancestors moved through life, experiencing the same common suffering (Layer 2) that we do.

Maintaining a relationship with our elders and ancestors helps anchor individuals and communities within a broader sense of continuity, wisdom, and identity. Elders carry lived knowledge—stories, cultural practices, and lessons learned through experience that can guide younger generations in navigating life's challenges and values. Honoring ancestors, whether through remembrance, storytelling, cultural traditions, or spiritual practices, reinforces a sense that we are part of an ongoing lineage rather than isolated individuals. This connection can foster humility, gratitude, and responsibility, reminding us that many of the opportunities and freedoms we experience were shaped by those who came before us. In turn, sustaining relationships with elders and honoring ancestors strengthens intergenerational bonds, preserves cultural memory, and helps communities carry forward knowledge, resilience, and care across time.

Epigenetics

Epigenetics is the study of how life experiences can influence the way genes are expressed, without changing the underlying DNA sequence. Environmental factors such as stress, nutrition, trauma, and social conditions can add chemical markers to genes that turn certain biological processes on or off. Research suggests that some of these epigenetic changes can be passed from one generation to the next, meaning that the experiences of our parents, grandparents, and even earlier ancestors may shape aspects of our biology, stress responses, and health vulnerabilities.[73] This perspective highlights that our bodies carry traces of historical and familial experiences, linking our personal well-being to the lives that came before us. At the same time, epigenetics also shows that these patterns are dynamic and responsive to the environment, suggesting that healing, supportive relationships, and healthier conditions can help reshape how genes are expressed across generations. We quite literally have the power to change future generations through our own healing. This is the ripple effect of internal work on a grand scale.

Practical Applications of Cultivating a Relationship with Elders and Ancestors

The following practices can help cultivate a stronger connection with our ancestors:

- Storytelling
- Learning family history
- Engaging in cultural or spiritual traditions
- Creating intentional rituals of remembrance
- Taking time to reflect on how their experiences, resilience, and wisdom live within us today
- Seeking support from elders

Individuals

For individuals, cultivating a relationship with elders and ancestors begins with recognizing that our lives are part of a much larger human story. Each person exists within a lineage shaped by generations of experiences, knowledge, struggles, and resilience. Taking time to learn about one's family history, cultural traditions, and ancestral practices can help individuals understand where they come from and how those histories have shaped their values, identities, and strengths. Practical ways to engage with this relationship include speaking with elders in one's family or community, listening to their stories, preserving traditions, researching family lineage, and participating in cultural rituals or remembrance practices that honor those who came before us. Some people create intentional practices such as keeping photographs, celebrating ancestral holidays, preparing traditional foods, or spending time reflecting on the lessons and sacrifices of prior generations. Engaging with ancestral wisdom in this way can deepen a sense of belonging, continuity, and gratitude while offering guidance for navigating present challenges.

Helping Professionals

Helping professionals can support this connection by encouraging clients to explore their cultural and ancestral backgrounds as potential sources of resilience and identity. Practitioners may invite clients to reflect on family narratives, cultural traditions, or values that have been passed down through generations. This can include asking questions about intergenerational strengths, coping strategies, and meaningful practices that have supported families or communities through hardship. In therapeutic or coaching settings, exploring ancestral context can also help clients understand patterns that exist across generations—both those that may create challenges and those that foster resilience. Helping professionals can create space for clients to reconnect with cultural heritage, honor family wisdom, and identify traditions that support a sense of grounding and belonging. When approached with cultural humility and sensitivity, this exploration can help individuals feel less isolated in their experiences and more connected to a broader lineage of human resilience.

Institutions and Policy

At the institutional and policy level, acknowledging the role of elders and ancestors means recognizing that intergenerational knowledge and cultural memory are powerful sources of resilience, identity, and community cohesion. Programs designed to support wellness, education, and community development can intentionally include opportunities for intergenerational engagement, storytelling, mentorship, and cultural knowledge sharing. Schools, community organizations, and healthcare systems can create spaces where elders are valued as carriers of wisdom and where younger generations are encouraged to learn from them. Policies that support cultural preservation, language revitalization, and community traditions also help sustain the transmission of ancestral knowledge. By integrating ancestral perspectives and honoring the role of elders in community life, institutions can strengthen social bonds, reinforce cultural identity, and cultivate collective resilience across generations.

CHAPTER 15:

Reimagining Relationship to Earth

Often we walk around unconscious to the fact that we live on this planet that provides everything we need to survive. There are many miracles to be found when we look closely at nature; even ourselves. Often we think of nature as something outside of ourselves, but we are also an integral part of the planet. Have you ever intentionally connected with nature and, all of a sudden, not felt as alone? This is because we are just another aspect of the nature we see as external to ourselves. We are quite literally connected—our bodies are made of the same matter that the rest of "nature" is made from. We go through the same cycles of birth, transformation, and death. We have deeply symbiotic relationships.

Human well-being is intimately intertwined with our relationship to planet Earth, as the environments we inhabit shape our mental, physical, emotional, and spiritual health. Natural systems provide the fundamental conditions for life—clean air, water, food, and climate stability—but they also nourish psychological and emotional balance. Research shows that time connecting with nature can reduce stress, improve mood, enhance cognitive functioning, and support physical health through movement and regulation of the nervous system. Beyond these measurable effects, many people experience the natural world as a source of meaning, belonging, and spiritual connection, reminding us that we are part of a larger living system rather than separate from it. When our relationship with the Earth becomes strained through environmental degradation or disconnection from natural spaces, both ecosystems and human health can suffer. Cultivating a respectful and reciprocal relationship with the planet through stewardship, awareness, and care can support not only ecological sustainability but also a deeper sense of personal and collective well-being.

Earth, Air, Fire & Water

Earth, air, fire, and water mirror the elements that make up our own bodies. The minerals and tissues that form our flesh arise from the same elements found in the soil; the air we breathe moves in and out of our lungs thousands of times each day, sustaining every cell; the electrical signals of our nervous system are tiny currents that coordinate sensation, movement, and thought, echoing the transformative energy symbolized by fire; and roughly 70 percent of the human body is composed of water. In this way, our bodies are not separate from the Earth but a living expression of it. Recognizing this connection may help explain why time spent in nature often brings a sense of calm and restoration. When we return to the natural world, we are reconnecting with the very elements that sustain and shape us.

Symbiotic Relationship with Plants & Animals

Humans exist in a deeply symbiotic relationship with the Earth, one in which our survival and well-being are intertwined with the living systems around us. The air we breathe is produced by plants and forests, the water that sustains our bodies cycles through ecosystems, and the soil that grows our food is maintained by complex networks of organisms. In return, human beings have long held roles as stewards of the land, shaping landscapes through cultivation, protection, and care. One of the most profound expressions of this relationship is found in plant medicines, which cultures around the world have used for thousands of years to support healing of the body, mind, and spirit. Many modern pharmaceuticals originate from plant compounds, and traditional healing systems have long recognized the therapeutic properties of herbs, roots, and fungi. These medicines reflect a reciprocal relationship: The Earth provides substances that can reduce suffering, regulate bodily systems, and support psychological or spiritual insight, while humans carry the responsibility to harvest, use, and protect these plants with respect and sustainability. Recognizing this reciprocity reminds us that our health is not separate from the health of the ecosystems that sustain us.

Humans also share a profound symbiotic relationship with animals, one that has shaped our survival, emotional lives, and cultures for thousands of years. Throughout human history, animals have provided companionship, protection, food, transportation, and assistance with work, while humans have offered care, shelter, and protection in return. Beyond these practical roles, relationships with animals can have meaningful effects on mental, emotional, and physical health. Research shows that interacting with animals can reduce stress hormones, lower blood pressure, increase feelings of connection, and support emotional regulation. Companion animals in particular often provide a sense of unconditional presence and attunement that can ease loneliness and foster feelings of safety and belonging. In many cultural and spiritual traditions, animals are also viewed as teachers or guides, reflecting qualities such as resilience, instinct, cooperation, and balance within ecosystems. Recognizing our connection with animals reminds us that we are part of a larger web of life, where mutual care, respect, and coexistence contribute to the well-being of both humans and the living world around us.

Awe

One of the things that nature can offer us is a sense of awe. Awe is the feeling that arises when we encounter something vast, beautiful, or profound that stretches our usual ways of understanding the world, such as standing beneath a star-filled sky, witnessing the power of nature, or experiencing moments of deep human connection. Psychologists describe awe as an emotion that expands our perspective and invites a sense of humility and wonder in the face of something larger than ourselves.[74] Research has shown that experiences of awe can have meaningful effects on wellness, including reducing stress, lowering inflammation, increasing feelings of connection with others, and promoting generosity and prosocial behavior. Awe can also quiet the constant self-focus that often accompanies anxiety or rumination, allowing people to feel more grounded, present, and connected to life. In this way, cultivating moments of awe through nature, art, spirituality, or meaningful experiences can support emotional balance, psychological resilience, and an expanded sense of meaning and belonging.

The following practices can help cultivate a stronger connection with the Earth.

- Working with plant medicines
- Connecting with animals
- Forest bathing
- Awe-inspiring experiences
- Gardening/growing food
- Tending to land
- Swimming in natural bodies of water
- Walking barefoot
- Nature-based play

Practical Application

Individuals

For individuals, cultivating a relationship with the Earth begins with recognizing that our well-being is closely tied to the natural environments that sustain us. Research consistently shows that time spent in nature can reduce stress, regulate the nervous system, improve mood, and support physical health. Practically, this means intentionally incorporating time outdoors into daily and weekly routines like walking in parks or forests, gardening, sitting near water, or simply pausing to notice the sky, plants, and changing seasons. Even small practices, such as tending to houseplants, grounding through barefoot contact with the soil, or taking mindful outdoor breaks, can help restore a sense of connection and balance. By acknowledging the impact that engaging with the Earth has on well-being and making these practices a regular part of life, individuals can cultivate a deeper sense of presence, gratitude, and belonging within the larger ecosystem.

Helping Professionals

Helping professionals can support this relationship by educating clients about the well-documented benefits of nature for mental, emotional, and physical health. Clinicians, coaches, and educators can encourage clients to incorporate nature-based practices into their self-care routines, such as walking outdoors during moments of stress, practicing mindfulness in natural environments, or engaging in activities like gardening or outdoor movement. In some contexts, professionals may also integrate nature directly into their work through outdoor sessions, nature-based reflection exercises, or encouraging clients to use natural settings as spaces for regulation and reflection. By normalizing and reinforcing the importance of connection with the natural world, helping professionals can empower clients to see the Earth not only as a resource, but also as a supportive partner in their healing and well-being.

Institutions and Policy

At the institutional and policy level, promoting connection with the Earth requires designing systems and environments that make nature accessible and valued as a component of public health. Institutions can incorporate language about environmental connection and nature engagement into wellness frameworks, recognizing that access to natural spaces contributes to mental and physical health outcomes. Schools, workplaces, and healthcare systems can intentionally create opportunities for outdoor learning, restorative breaks, and nature-based programming. Urban planning and institutional design can prioritize green spaces, gardens, natural light, and access to parks and trails. Policies that support time away from dense urban environments such as flexible scheduling, outdoor programming, and retreats can also encourage individuals to reconnect with nature. By intentionally integrating natural environments into wellness initiatives and public infrastructure, institutions help cultivate communities where both people and ecosystems can thrive together.

CHAPTER 16:

Integration of Embodied Awareness

As we move from the practical application of relationships with the various parts of ourselves toward a broader understanding of the many elements that shape the human experience, we begin to explore how engaging and integrating the full range of our senses can deepen our capacity for insight and awareness. When we allow ourselves to fully perceive, feel, and interpret the signals available to us, both external and internal, we cultivate a more expansive form of knowing. This deeper awareness brings us closer to understanding ourselves with greater clarity and aligning more fully with our purpose and meaning.

For much of modern history, human perception has been described as operating through five primary senses: sight, hearing, touch, taste, and smell. These senses allow us to navigate the physical world, gather information about our surroundings, and make decisions that support survival. Yet, while these sensory channels are powerful, they represent only a portion of how human beings experience reality. When we rely exclusively on these external senses, we may begin to assume that what we can directly see, hear, or measure is the full extent of what exists. In doing so, we risk overlooking the more subtle ways that humans perceive, process, and understand the world.

In addition to the traditional five senses, human experience includes a range of internal and intuitive forms of perception. One of the most widely recognized of these is intuition, often described as a felt sense of knowing that arises without conscious reasoning. Intuition can appear as a bodily sensation, a sudden insight, or a quiet inner awareness that helps guide decisions and responses. Neuroscience and psychology increasingly recognize that intuitive processes arise from complex integrations of past experiences, pattern recognition, and subconscious processing. While intuition may feel mysterious, it often reflects the brain's ability to synthesize information in ways that occur outside of conscious awareness. It is often felt in the body.

Across many contemplative and spiritual traditions, additional intuitive capacities have been described through what are often called the "clairs"—a term derived from the French word for "clear." These include experiences such as clairvoyance (clear seeing or visual insight), clairaudience (clear hearing or inner auditory perception), clairsentience (clear feeling or emotional sensing), and claircognizance (clear knowing). While these concepts are interpreted differently across cultures and individuals, they broadly refer to the ways people sometimes experience information, insight, or awareness that does not arise directly through the five physical senses.

Regardless of how one interprets these experiences—whether through spiritual, psychological, or symbolic frameworks, they highlight an important truth: Human perception is layered and multidimensional. Beyond the external senses, we also possess interoception (awareness of internal bodily states), emotional perception, imagination, memory, and intuition. These capacities allow us to detect subtle shifts in our environment, relationships, and inner life. When we learn to pay attention to these signals, we gain access to a richer and more nuanced understanding of ourselves and the world around us.

Developing sensitivity to these forms of perception requires presence and practice. Modern life often encourages constant stimulation, distraction, and reliance on external data. In contrast, intuitive awareness tends to emerge in moments of stillness, reflection, and embodied attention. It requires us to ask ourselves, "What do I need to know that I don't know right now?" and to then truly listen for an answer. We often feel confused or unsure about what to do in our lives, but truly, we do know. Instead of looking outside of ourselves for answers, we just have to take a moment to ask ourselves, tune into the stillness and a regulated nervous system, and sense the spirit's and body's cues. Practices that have been highlighted in previous chapters, such as meditation, time in nature, creative expression, breathwork, and contemplative inquiry can help individuals become more attuned to subtle sensations and insights that might otherwise be overlooked. Rather than replacing rational thinking, these practices complement analytical understanding with experiential wisdom.

When we begin to acknowledge both our sensory and intuitive capacities, our experience of reality can expand. We may become more attuned to emotional dynamics in relationships, more aware of signals from our own bodies, and more responsive to the environments we inhabit. This broader awareness can support more aligned decision-making, deeper empathy, and a greater sense of connection with others and the world around us. Just as we experience the benefits of Wi-Fi or cellular signals that we can't see, we can experience the benefits of our invisible "clairs."

Living in our full reality does not mean abandoning science, reason, or the five senses. Instead, it means recognizing that human perception operates across multiple layers (physical, emotional, cognitive, and intuitive). By honoring all of these dimensions, we move beyond a narrow view of experience and begin to engage with life in a more integrated and holistic way. In doing so, we cultivate a deeper relationship with ourselves, with others, and with the complex reality of which we inhabit.

Practical Application

Individuals

Cultivate practices that help reconnect with both external and internal perception. This can include many practices that have already been discussed: mindfulness meditation, breath awareness, somatic practices, and time in nature, all of which can help you become more attuned to bodily sensations, emotional signals, and intuitive insights. Journaling, creative expression, and reflective practices can also support individuals in noticing subtle forms of perception such as intuition or emotional resonance. Learning to pause and check in with the body, asking questions like *What am I sensing?* or *What feels aligned or misaligned?* or *What do I need to know?* can strengthen the ability to integrate intellectual reasoning with embodied awareness. Over time, these practices help individuals make decisions that feel more congruent with their values, needs, and sense of purpose.

Helping Professionals

Support clients in expanding their sensory awareness by creating spaces that encourage curiosity, safety, and embodied exploration. One practical approach is helping clients develop greater interoceptive awareness—the ability to notice internal sensations such as breath, tension, warmth, or shifts in energy. Techniques like mindfulness, grounding exercises, body scans, and slow breathing can help clients reconnect with signals from their nervous system and body. Professionals can also invite clients to reflect on subtle cues such as gut feelings, emotional shifts, or imagery that arises during conversation, helping them differentiate between reactive impulses and deeper intuitive insight. Importantly, helping professionals guide clients to integrate these insights with thoughtful reflection and evidence-based coping strategies, ensuring that intuitive awareness complements rather than replaces critical thinking. Through this process, clients can develop a more integrated relationship with their thoughts, emotions, bodily sensations, and intuitive signals, allowing them to make decisions and navigate life with greater clarity and self-trust. In helping professions especially, the absence of intuitive awareness can reduce attunement—professionals may overlook subtle emotional or relational cues that are critical for effective care.

Institutions and Policy

Institutions and organizations can support integrated and embodied awareness by expanding their language to include intuition as a valid and valuable source of information. Much of institutional culture prioritizes what can be measured and observed, often overlooking the internal signals people use to navigate their lives—gut feelings, inner knowing, emotional resonance, and subtle bodily cues. Promoting language that reflects the full human experience means normalizing questions like: *What is your intuition telling you?* or *What feels aligned or off?* or *What are you sensing beneath the surface?* alongside more traditional, cognitive assessments.

This shift does not replace evidence-based approaches, but complements them by recognizing that individuals often perceive important information before they can logically explain it. Institutions can reinforce this by creating spaces and practices that encourage pausing, reflecting, and listening inward, whether through brief check-ins, quiet environments, or contemplative practices. Training leaders and professionals to attend to both observable data and intuitive cues such as shifts in tone, energy, or body language further supports this integration.

By acknowledging intuition as part of how humans understand themselves and the world, institutions foster environments where people feel more fully engaged, self-aware, and aligned—supporting not just performance, but deeper clarity, trust, and whole-person well-being.

When intuition is ignored, individuals often become disconnected from an important internal guidance system, relying solely on external validation, logic, or institutional expectations to make decisions. Over time, this can lead to a sense of misalignment—people may follow paths that look "right" on paper but feel off internally, resulting in confusion, burnout, or a lack of fulfillment. Without access to intuitive signals, early indicators of stress, boundary violations, or misfit environments are often missed, meaning issues are only addressed once they become more acute or disruptive.

At a broader level, when institutions ignore intuition, they tend to over-rely on standardization and surface-level metrics, which can miss the deeper realities of human experience. This can contribute to environments where individuals feel unseen, where relational dynamics go unaddressed, and where decision-making lacks nuance or responsiveness. Ultimately, ignoring intuition can lead to a culture that is disconnected, where people are functioning but not fully engaged or aligned. Reintegrating intuition helps restore balance, allowing individuals and systems to respond not just to what is visible and measurable, but to what is felt, sensed, and known beneath the surface.

CHAPTER 17:

Unraveling and Creation

Toward Knowledge, Wisdom and Meaning

"As far as we can discern, the sole purpose of human existence is to kindle a light of meaning in the darkness of mere being." —Carl Jung, *Memories, Dreams, Reflections*

During a plant medicine journey, as I was going through the process of ego disintegration, I said to my guide, "I think I'm going crazy; I can't go crazy—my kids need me." And he whispered in my ear, "It's okay to go crazy once in a while—it won't last forever." That statement was revolutionary for me. How often do we get permission to totally lose it, to dissolve into a messy, chaotic form that has no clear indicator if or when it might reform into something functional? That's scary—for both the person going through it, for those around them, and for society. But it is wholly necessary for a radical transformation to occur.

Nature as an Example

This layer of the Human Experience Labyrinth is often the messiest and most prone to being pathologized. Disintegration and the process of being slowly rebuilt is uncomfortable and scary for both the person experiencing it and those around them. However, just like the butterfly reorganizing and then emerging from its cocoon, the struggle is an integral component of the transformation.

Throughout the natural world, life unfolds in an ongoing cycle of birth, growth, death, and rebirth. Forests shed leaves each autumn so that new life can emerge in the spring. Rivers flood and recede, reshaping the land over time. Stars collapse and reform in distant galaxies, and ecosystems continually reorganize themselves through seasons of expansion, decay, and renewal. Nothing in nature remains fixed; transformation is not an exception to life's processes but one of its defining features. These cycles remind us that what appears to be an ending is often a necessary stage in the creation of something new.

Human development follows a similar rhythm. Periods of growth and expansion are often preceded by moments when familiar identities, beliefs, or ways of living begin to break down. Yet in many modern contexts, these transitional phases are frequently misunderstood. Emotional upheaval, questioning of old frameworks, or temporary disorientation can be quickly labeled as dysfunction rather than recognized as a natural stage of transformation. When viewed through the lens of pathology alone, the process of expansion may appear as something that needs to be corrected or suppressed. When we witness a path that looks like an unorganized expression of expansion and contraction, we feel that something is not going right. We want to see a clear path of "improvement." When we reflect on our most basic form of creation—giving birth—we see that there is most definitely contraction and expansion. Being stuck in a state of contraction or in a state of expansion would not allow for the process to take place. Seeing the necessary contraction and expansion as expected and known aspects of transformation creates a softness and spaciousness that this process requires.

Nature offers this perspective so beautifully. Just as a seed must split open before it can grow into a plant, human transformation often requires a phase where old structures dissolve. This does not mean that every experience of distress is purely transformative, nor that support and care are unnecessary. Rather, it suggests that some periods of difficulty may represent movement within a larger cycle of development. When these experiences are held within supportive environments that allow expression, reflection, and integration, they can become gateways to deeper understanding rather than signs of failure.

Normalizing this cyclical process invites a more compassionate view of change. Instead of assuming that stability is the only healthy state, we begin to recognize that periods of disruption can be part of growth. Just as the Earth continually renews itself through cycles of decay and regeneration, human beings also evolve through phases of breakdown and reorganization. When we align our understanding of personal development with the rhythms of the natural world, transformation becomes less of something to fear and more of something to navigate with patience, curiosity, and care.

In this way, expansion is not an anomaly; it is part of the same creative process that shapes forests, oceans, ecosystems, and stars. Recognizing this can help shift our perspective from pathologizing change to honoring the profound intelligence within life's cycles of renewal.

Metamorphosis

When a caterpillar enters the chrysalis, it does not simply grow wings; it undergoes a profound biological dissolution. Inside the chrysalis, much of the caterpillar's body breaks down into a kind of cellular "soup." Within this seeming disintegration, specialized cells, often called imaginal cells, begin organizing a completely new structure, eventually forming the butterfly. This stage is not gentle or orderly; it is a period of complete reorganization where the old form must dissolve so that a new one can emerge.

The final stage of this process offers an important lesson about growth and resilience. When the butterfly is ready to emerge, it must struggle to push itself out of the chrysalis through a small opening. This effort is not accidental; it is essential. The pressure of squeezing through the narrow space forces fluid from the butterfly's abdomen into its wings, allowing them to expand and strengthen so that it can fly. If someone intervenes and cuts open the chrysalis to "help" the butterfly emerge, the butterfly often survives only briefly. Without the struggle that strengthens its wings, it cannot fly and is left vulnerable.

This process illustrates an important truth about transformation: Struggle is sometimes part of development rather than a sign that something has gone wrong. In the same way that the butterfly's effort is necessary for its survival, human growth often includes periods of difficulty, uncertainty, and internal reorganization. When these moments are immediately interrupted, suppressed, or pathologized, we may unintentionally interfere with processes that are meant to build strength, resilience, and new capacities.

The butterfly's transformation reminds us that emergence often requires tension, effort, and time. What appears from the outside to be a struggle that the person may not survive, may actually be the very mechanism through which new life becomes possible.

This does not mean that people should face hardship alone or without support. Just as the butterfly benefits from the protective structure of the chrysalis during its transformation, humans also need safe environments, guidance, and care during periods of change. The key distinction is between supporting the process and prematurely rescuing someone from it with numbing substances or focusing on just one part of the Labyrinth, such as coping skills, instead of acknowledging the entirety of the human experience. Support provides safety while allowing growth to unfold naturally. This is why the implementation and integration of all of the practices and approaches to assist an individual in their human experience journey are vitally important. Without the full vision of the human experience and a supportive and comprehensive container for one to move through the various layers required for expansive transformation, they are likely to become too overwhelmed, contract, and need to receive interventions that return a feeling of safety, but stunt their opportunity for growth. The more we can create communities and societies that embrace this process and offer support as a way of existing, rather than focus on interventions for people who are in the part of the journey that is outwardly distressing, the more we allow for individuals to expand. And the more we allow for expansion, the more their families, co-workers, and communities will benefit. This is how we change the world.

How Can We Support AND Allow for Distress During Metamorphosis?

When we not only don't see the value in the struggle, but intentionally try to remove it, we eliminate the perceived need for wise elders and relational support. We, as a society, have lost our connection with community and elder support and therefore don't know how to sit with someone in distress, while also providing a supportive presence.

Holding Space vs. Rescuing

Holding Space / Community Support	Swooping In / Rescuing
Recognizes that sadness, grief, and even periods of depression can be normal human responses	Treats sadness or distress as something that must be immediately fixed or eliminated
Allows the person to feel their emotions fully, without judgment	Attempts to stop or distract from emotions quickly (e.g., "Don't feel that way," "Stay positive")
Says: "I'm here with you in this"	Says (implicitly or explicitly): "This shouldn't be happening—let's make it go away"
Focuses on presence over solutions	Focuses on solutions over presence
Trusts the individual's capacity to move through their experience	Assumes the person cannot handle their experience without intervention
Offers attunement and listening—not needing to change what is happening	Interrupts or redirects the experience to reduce discomfort (for them or for the helper)
Supports without taking over: "What do you need right now?"	Takes control: "Here's what you should do"
Normalizes: "It makes sense you feel this way given what you've been through"	Pathologizes: "Something is wrong—you shouldn't feel like this"
Holds boundaries + care (staying present while not absorbing or fixing)	Can lead to over-involvement or dependency
Encourages integration and meaning-making over time	Prioritizes quick relief, sometimes at the expense of deeper processing
Makes space for silence, tears, and uncertainty	Fills space to avoid discomfort (advice, reassurance, distraction)
Sees sadness as something that can coexist with care and connection	Sees sadness as something that must be replaced with happiness

Important Nuances

Ignoring suffering is leaving someone who is struggling, alone. We aim not to ignore suffering, but rather to provide support. To

feel supported, the person must be seen, heard and tended to. If someone is at risk, unsafe, or unable to function, intervention can be necessary. But outside of crisis, many emotional experiences are meant to be felt, witnessed, and integrated, not removed immediately. Leaning into allowing for expression of emotions is how we soften them. When my son passed over, I lost my mind. I needed help, but often what we find is that nothing can help the process of sadness. It's not a disease that can just be fixed with medicine. It is something that needs to be processed. I needed supportive people near me, checking on me, holding me, and listening to me. I did not need people telling me what to do to feel better—trying to get me out of the house, moving my body, socializing, etc. I needed to be in my process and be told that it's okay and normal that I was losing my mind, that I was in a grief bubble, and that I didn't want to socialize or move my body. Being reminded that it wouldn't last forever—while allowing for it without resistance—is the only medicine that worked.

And funny enough, at the same time that I was experiencing this, I was witnessing my other son go into a deep, dissociated depression. And it killed me to witness it. But I knew, because I was in it myself, that there was nothing that could be done outside of allowing for it, tending to him, normalizing it, and seeking helpers who could help him feel resourced enough to slowly begin moving the massive feelings through his body. I had learned a very hard lesson from my oldest son's passing—I had tried to get rid of his depression. I was so uncomfortable with it and felt pressure from the outside world to get him on medication, that I created an environment of resistance to allowing for his big emotions. He felt scared that he was having such big emotions and didn't know how to hold or feel them. Instead of focusing on resourcing him (we did do some of this with therapy, but if I'm being honest the goal was to make him feel better, not build capacity and meaning-making), we medicated him. Side effects from this medication, and the despair he felt when it wasn't working, is what ultimately led to his death. In 2023, 53 percent of high school youth reported having felt sad or hopeless, seriously considered suicide, made a suicide plan, or attempted suicide. Self-reported rates of suicidal thoughts, plans, and attempts were higher among high school youth than among adults in general.[75] Fearing conversations about suicide instead of normalizing this common thought created an environment of resistance to feeling those emotions, which only made them bigger. I cannot emphasize this enough—witnessing, listening to, normalizing, and caring for someone who is going through an emotional crisis is extremely challenging *and* wholly necessary. There is no "easy fix." This is part of the very normal human experience that must be held by community.

Attuning to people and allowing for expression of emotion allows:

- People to build emotional capacity
- People to feel seen instead of corrected
- People to develop trust in themselves
- Communities to become places of real connection, not just problem-solving

The Journey: Surrender to Integration of Knowledge, Knowing, and Feeling

Growth rarely arrives in a tidy or linear way. Much of the journey toward knowledge, wisdom, and meaning unfolds in a period of unraveling—a phase that can feel disorienting, messy, and deeply uncomfortable. When individuals begin to question long-held beliefs, confront painful experiences, or open themselves to deeper self-awareness, the structures that once organized their lives may begin to loosen or dissolve. In a culture that often prioritizes control, certainty, and emotional comfort, this process can easily be misunderstood or pathologized. Feelings such as sadness, confusion, grief, or depression are often treated as problems to eliminate immediately rather than signals that a deeper transformation may be unfolding.

The impulse to quickly remove or suppress so-called "negative" emotions is understandable. These feelings can be heavy, unfamiliar and, at times, frightening. Yet when we rush to silence them, we may also interrupt the natural alchemy of emotional and psychological transformation. Just as physical wounds require time to heal, emotional and existential wounds often move through phases of expression, release, and integration. When supported with care and understanding, these experiences can become catalysts for deeper clarity and growth, rather than conditions that must simply be "fixed."

Allowing emotions to move through their natural progression requires a willingness to permit disintegration—to let certain identities, assumptions, or ways of being, fall apart. This stage can feel chaotic, as though the ground beneath us is shifting. It is often during this period that individuals encounter what some traditions call a spiritual crisis or metamorphosis. Old frameworks for understanding life may no longer fit, yet new ones have not fully formed. The result can feel like standing between worlds: the past dissolving, the future not yet visible.

Importantly, this stage is not meant to last forever. Transformation is not an endless process of digging through pain or remaining indefinitely in states of introspection. The purpose of confronting and expressing previously unprocessed emotions is to allow them to move through the system so they no longer create harm or stagnation. When emotions are acknowledged and allowed to flow, they lose their grip. When stories rooted in fear, shame, or limitation are examined and released, they no longer define our actions. Through education, insight, and experience, individuals begin to approach life's challenges with a new framework, one that allows feelings to arise and move through rather than becoming trapped within them.

This process can feel messy because it requires surrender—not resignation, but the willingness to soften our grip on rigid identities and defenses. Surrender allows knowledge, knowing, and feeling to integrate. Intellectual understanding alone rarely creates lasting transformation; it must be paired with lived experience and emotional and physical integration. When these elements begin to align, individuals often discover a deeper form of wisdom that cannot be accessed through thought alone.

In this sense, the unraveling process is not the opposite of aligning with meaning, it is often the path toward it. Finding meaning does not mean the absence of difficulty or the avoidance of painful emotions. Rather, it emerges when we are no longer controlled by the stories, fears, or unprocessed experiences that once shaped our perception of life. As old patterns dissolve and new perspectives emerge, individuals may find themselves relating to their emotions, relationships, and circumstances with greater clarity and spaciousness.

Eventually, the period of metamorphosis gives way to creation. With old structures cleared, individuals begin to construct lives rooted in deeper awareness and intention. Decisions may become more aligned with values and purpose. Relationships may grow more authentic. Emotional experiences may still arise, but they are met with curiosity and compassion rather than resistance. Life regains its forward movement.

We are not sitting on the spiritual pot forever! The goal of this work is not to remain perpetually in a state of introspection or spiritual searching. The purpose is to return to life more fully, carrying the wisdom gained from the journey. We may go through this iteration multiple times; as the Labyrinth shows us, the path continues, and each time we return to a familiar part of the path, we enter into it with a new, clearer way of being. Each time we learn more and can engage on a deeper level. The clearing of old energies and the integration of new understanding allows individuals to engage with the world with greater peace, creativity, and joy. What once felt like darkness becomes the soil from which meaning grows.

In this way, the messy process of unraveling becomes part of the deeper human task that Jung described as "kindling a light of meaning in the darkness of mere being."[76] Through the willingness to face discomfort, allow transformation, and integrate what we learn, we participate in the ongoing creation of a life that reflects both our suffering and our capacity for joy, meaning, and wisdom.

Practical Application

Individuals

For individuals, the most important step in this phase is understanding that disintegration is often part of transformation. When people begin to question old beliefs, feel emotions that were previously suppressed, or loosen their attachment to identities that once defined them, it can feel as though parts of the self are dissolving. This experience can be frightening because the mind naturally seeks stability and certainty. Yet, what may feel like something inside of us "dying" is often the shedding of structures that no longer serve our growth.

This stage invites individuals to allow the work from all aspects of the human experience—mental, emotional, physical, relational, and spiritual—to begin integrating into the whole of who they are. Insights gained through reflection, healing, and self-awareness gradually move from intellectual understanding into embodied wisdom. Rather than resisting this process or attempting to quickly return to comfort, individuals can practice leaning into it with curiosity and compassion. Surrender in this context does not mean giving up; it means trusting the process of transformation enough to allow it to unfold.

During these periods, it is helpful to remember that transformation often feels messy and uncertain before clarity emerges. Emotions may fluctuate, identities may shift, and the future may feel temporarily unclear. Yet these experiences are frequently signs that something new is forming. By allowing space for the process, continuing practices that support connection to the body, emotions, community, nature, and meaning, individuals create the conditions for a more integrated and authentic version of themselves to emerge.

Helping Professionals

Helping professionals play an important role in supporting individuals through these transformative stages. One powerful way to do this is by helping clients understand where they may be within the broader journey of the human experience. When individuals are in a period of unraveling or reorganization, they may interpret their experience as failure, instability, or something being "wrong" with them. Helping professionals can normalize this stage by explaining that transformation often includes phases of uncertainty, emotional intensity, and re-evaluation of previously held beliefs. They can point them toward Layer 6 of the Labyrinth and help them see how close they are to transformation.

Rather than focusing solely on strategies to quickly reduce discomfort, practitioners can help clients develop the capacity to remain present with the process. This includes encouraging practices that support regulation, grounding, and reflection, while also helping clients understand that meaningful change often requires moving through discomfort rather than avoiding it. Professionals can gently remind clients that the chaos they are experiencing may be part of a larger restructuring that leads to greater clarity, resilience, and purpose.

At the same time, practitioners provide an important part of the container that allows this work to unfold safely. By offering empathy, perspective, and practical tools, they help clients feel supported as they navigate the uncertainty of transformation. Reminding clients that there is often something meaningful and expansive on the other side of the mess can help cultivate hope and trust in the process.

Institutions and Policy

At the institutional and policy level, supporting this aspect of the human experience requires shifting cultural narratives about growth and well-being. Many systems emphasize stability, productivity, and rapid solutions, often leaving little room for the natural cycles of questioning, transformation, and renewal that individuals experience throughout life. Institutions can play a critical role in normalizing the full range of human development by acknowledging that periods of transition, emotional intensity, and identity exploration are natural parts of growth.

This can be reflected in language, programming, and policy that support whole-person development. Educational systems, workplaces, and healthcare organizations can create environments where reflection, mentorship, mental health support, and community dialogue are encouraged. Policies that allow time and space for personal development, such as sabbaticals, wellness programs, or community support initiatives, recognize that transformation is part of living a meaningful life.

By acknowledging that the human journey includes phases of unraveling and renewal, institutions help shift the narrative from one that pathologizes struggle to one that recognizes transformation as a normal and often necessary part of becoming. In doing so, systems can better support individuals as they move toward deeper knowledge, wisdom, and meaning in their lives, that will ultimately benefit the organization and community.

CHAPTER 18:

Closing Thoughts

The Courage to Hold the Whole Story

We find ourselves at an important moment in time—a crossroads in how we understand and respond to human suffering. For decades, mental health care has advanced through clinical knowledge, research, and expanding access to treatment. These developments have saved lives and must continue. Yet alongside these practical tools, deeper questions are emerging: *What is the true goal of mental health care? Is it simply to reduce discomfort, or is it to help human beings navigate the full terrain of their lives—suffering, transformation, connection, and meaning?*

As we move toward what could be called a Post Pathology Era, we are invited not only to refine our interventions but to expand our paradigm. The Human Experience Labyrinth offers one way of seeing this broader journey: a reminder that life unfolds through cycles of confusion, growth, loss, integration, and renewal. Within this orientation, the aim of care is not merely comfort but meaning. Meaning > Comfort because meaning allows individuals and communities to carry suffering in ways that lead to wisdom, participation, and resilience.

This shift cannot occur within clinics or policy frameworks alone. The work cannot be outsourced. Mental health is not only the responsibility of professionals; it is a shared human task that lives within individuals, families, communities, and cultures. The ways we interpret pain, growth, identity, and healing shape the systems we build around them. In truth, systems reflect belief. If we believe human distress is only pathology, our systems will attempt to correct and contain it. If we recognize that distress can also be part of growth, transformation, and meaning-making, our systems will begin to support navigation rather than correction alone. This requires both/and thinking—holding the necessity of clinical care alongside the deeper processes through which people integrate their experiences, find belonging, and reconnect with purpose.

Throughout history, cultures have relied not only on healers but also on wise elders—individuals who carried lived experience, perspective, and the ability to contextualize suffering within a larger story of life. Reclaiming this balance means expanding mental health care beyond symptom management toward communities capable of holding the full arc of human experience. When individuals begin to orient themselves within the Labyrinth—learning from the ego, engaging their bodies, connecting with all parts of themselves and others, and seeking meaning—they do not only change themselves, they change the environments around them. Families become more reflective, communities become more compassionate, and systems slowly evolve.

The invitation of this moment is both simple and profound: to participate in this shift. To examine our assumptions about suffering, healing, and growth. To move toward a culture where mental health care supports not only stability, but wisdom. When individuals begin to walk this path, the ripple effects extend far beyond personal well-being. They shape conversations in homes, influence how professionals practice, and ultimately reshape the systems we collectively create.

The crossroads before us is not only a challenge, it is an exciting opportunity. If we are willing to embrace it, we can help cultivate a future in which mental health care reflects the fullness of human life: one where suffering is met with compassion, growth is supported with courage, and meaning becomes the compass guiding us through the Labyrinth together.

We must learn to walk the Labyrinth with one another. Not to eliminate the twists and turns, but to help each other move through them, emerging with deeper knowledge, wisdom, and meaning.

Let's Not Analyze The Joy Out of Existence

While there is certainly much hard work to be done as we move through the Labyrinth, I believe understanding where we are in the Human Experience Labyrinth will help us to zoom out and understand that we do not need to spend so much time contemplating our suffering. If we simply understand it as a natural and normal part of our existence, the vast amount of emotional, mental, and physical energy we devote to analyzing our traumas, our diagnosis, our ego response ... can dissipate. By simply acknowledging the normalcy of the human experience, letting go of our pathology, we can lean into our current circumstances instead of resist. And when we let go of resistance, we soften and find more energy and room for lightness and joy. This is the feedback loop we want to encourage.

The simple act of acknowledging the human experience over pathologizing it is immensely powerful and is the first ripple in the pond of transformation. I wonder how orienting my parenting toward this framework would have changed Noah's internal dialogue, pressure, and distress. I wonder how using the framework to intentionally strengthen Noah's relationships with himself, community, and something greater would have altered his path. Noah's legacy is one of hope, love, connection, and deep meaning. Noah's life and physical death have transformed me. He has shown me the importance of connection—with all of the parts of ourselves, with community, and with something greater. He has shown me how our individual work is the only way to create the ripple effect of change. It is impossible to impact a change in others if we do not embody that change within ourselves. In my quest to understand how I can ensure that my living children, other families, and I, myself, do not feel the despair and hopelessness that Noah felt, I have discovered that change starts from within. I can't help my children or my community until I can embody, take action, and live my life in alignment with the inner layers and core of the Labyrinth.

As I'm writing this, my seven-year-old neighbor came to visit me on the porch. I'm in the middle of final edits and have a timeline I'm trying to adhere to. I set my computer aside and was present with him. Engaged with him. Answered his questions. Asked him questions. I saw a little version of Noah in him. This is the best and highest use of our time. True, meaningful connection. Building the foundation that holds the potential for a deeper relationship that can be supportive to him as he grows and moves through his inherent and predictable life challenges. The book will get done. I don't know the next time he'll want to connect with me.

Every genuine interaction a person has with another human is mental health care.

Every time someone feels seen and cared for in community is suicide prevention.

Every time a person sees their struggle and meaning-making process reflected in another human and in society as "normal," we reduce suffering.

Every time we are encouraged to fully feel instead of "get better," we reduce the likelihood of disease and harmful expressions of emotion.

When we can see ourselves as moving through the Labyrinth with intention and meaning, we find lightness, gratitude, and joy as part of the wholeness of the human experience.

We are not alone.

We are in this human experience together, for a reason.

For a PDF with integration prompts, exercises, and practical steps to explore and expand each of the seven layers—for personal development, helping professionals, and organizations, scan the QR code or visit **drtiffanyryan.org.**

Notes

1. Friedrich Nietzsche, *Götzen-Dämmerung; oder, Wie man mit dem Hammer philosophirt* (C.G. Naumann, 1889), quoted in Victor E. Frankl, *Man's Search for Meaning*, translated by Ilse Lasch (Beacon Press, 2006).

2. Edith Weisskopf-Joelson quoted in Frankl, *Man's Search for Meaning*.

3. Frankl, *Man's Search for Meaning*.

4. Jon Kabat-Zinn, *Wherever You Go, There You Are: Mindfulness Meditation in Everyday Life* (Hyperion, 1994).

5. "Person in environment" is foundational to the social work profession, widely used. Jane Adams is considered the pioneer for this term and social work.

6. Gordon Allport, preface to *Man's Search for Meaning*.

7. Frankl, *Man's Search for Meaning*.

8. Frankl, *Man's Search for Meaning*.

9. R.G. Tedeschi & L.G. Calhoun, "Posttraumatic growth inventory," *Journal of Traumatic Stress 9*, no. 3 (1996): 455–471.

10. Jalal al-Din Rumi, "Birdwings," *The Essential Rumi*, trans. Coleman Barks and John Moyne (HarperOne, 1995).

11. Ram Dass and Stephen Levine, *Grist for the Mill: Awakening to Oneness* (HarperOne, (2014).

12. Tiffany Ryan, *Soul Work: A Field Guide to Freedom* (Synergy Publishing Group, 2025). In my previous book, *soul work* is defined as teachings that support emotional healing, conscious living, and personal freedom in my book.

13. DailyShaman, Facebook, January 23, 2026, "This affirms the sacredness ...," https://www.facebook.com/share/p/1CztyYhkV7/.

14. Elisabeth Kübler-Ross, *On Death and Dying* (The Macmillan Company, 1969).

15. Dennis Klass, Phyllis Silverman, and Steven L. Nickman, ed., *Continuing Bonds: New Understandings of Grief* (Taylor & Francis, 1996).

16. Non-medical professionals that provide emotional, spiritual, and practical support to terminally ill patients and their families, offering services such as vigil planning, companionship, and respite care to improve quality of life.

17. Hsueh-Han Yeh, Joslyn Westphal, Yong Hu, Edward L. Peterson, L. Keoki Williams, Deepak Prabhakar, Cathrine Frank, et al, "Diagnosed Mental Health Conditions and Risk of Suicide Mortality," *Psychiatric Services* 70, no. 9 (September 2019): 750–57, doi:10.1176/appi.ps.201800346.

18. Alina Surís, Ryan Holliday, and Carol S. North, "The evolution of the classification of psychiatric disorders," *Behavioral Sciences* 6, no. 1 (2016): 5, https://doi.org/10.3390/bs6010005.

19. "What Is Solution-Focused Therapy?" Institute for Solution-Focused Therapy, accessed May 21, 2026, https://solutionfocused.net/what-is-solution-focused-therapy/.

20. Steve Taylor, "Breakdowns and 'Shift-Ups,'" *Psychology Today*, published February 12, 2016, https://www.psychologytoday.com/us/blog/out-the-darkness/201602/breakdowns-and-shift-ups.

21. "Why Culturally Sensitive Care for Indigenous Populations with Schizophrenia Matters," PsychCentral, last medically reviewed October 29, 2021, https://psychcentral.com/schizophrenia/schizophrenia-indigenous.

22. Kao-Ping Chua, Anna Volerman, Jason Zhang, Joanna Hua, and Rena Conti, "Antidepressant dispensing to U.S. adolescents and young adults: 2016–202," *Pediatrics* 153, no. 3 (2024): e2023064245, https://doi.org/10.1542/peds.2023-064245.

23. Debra J. Brody and Jeffery P. Hughes, "Depression prevalence in adolescents and adults: United States, August 2021–August 2023," *NCHS Data Brief* no. 527 (April 2025), National Center for Health Statistics, https://doi.org/10.15620/cdc/174579.

24. Emily P. Terlizzi and Benjamin Zablotsky, "Symptoms of anxiety and depression among adults: United States, 2019 and 2022," National Health Statistics Reports, no. 213 (2024), https://doi.org/10.15620/cdc/64018.

25. "Suicide Data and Statistics," Suicide Prevention, Centers for Disease Control and Prevention, updated March 26, 2025, https://www.cdc.gov/suicide/facts/data.html.

26. Jeffrey R. Lacasse and Jonathan Leo, "Serotonin and depression: A disconnect between advertisements and the scientific literature," *PLoS Medicine 2*, no. 12 (2005): e392, https://doi.org/10.1371/journal.pmed.0020392.

27. Joanna Moncrieff, Ruth E. Cooper, Tom Stochmann, et al., "The serotonin theory of depression: A systematic umbrella review," *Molecular*

Psychiatry 28, no. 3242–3256 (2023), https://doi.org/10.1038/s41380-022-01661-0

28. "Analysis: Depression probably not caused by chemical imbalance in brain—new study," University College London, published July 20, 2022, https://www.ucl.ac.uk/news/2022/jul/analysis-depression-probably-not-caused-chemical-imbalance-brain-new-study. Article references the study cited above in *Molecular Psychiatry.*

29. Andrea Cipriani et al., "Comparative efficacy and acceptability of 21 antidepressant drugs for the acute treatment of adults with major depressive disorder: a system review and network meta-analysis," *Lancet* 391, no. 10128 (2018), 1357–1366, doi:10.1016/S0140-6736(17)32802-7.

30. Irving Kirsch, et al., "Initial severity and antidepressant benefits: a meta-analysis of data submitted to the Food and Drug Administration," *PLoS Medicine* 5, no. 2(2008): e45, doi:10.1371/journal.pmed.0050045; and J.C. Jakobsen, K.K. Katakam, A. Schou, et al., "Erratum to: Selective serotonin reuptake inhibitors versus placebo in patients with major depressive disorder. A systematic review with meta-analysis and Trial Sequential Analysis," *BMC Psychiatry* 17, no. 162 (2017), https://doi.org/10.1186/s12888-017-1311-5.

31. Giovanni A. Fava et al., "Withdrawal symptoms after Selective Serotonin Reuptake Inhibitor Discontinuation: A Systemic Review," *Psychotherapy and Psychosomatics* 84, no. 2 (2015): 72–81, doi:10.1159/000370338.

32. "Suicidality in children and adolescents being treated with antidepressant medications," U.S. Food and Drug Administration, last updated February 5, 2018, https://www.fda.gov/drugs/postmarket-drug-safety-information-patients-and-providers/suicidality-children-and-adolescents-being-treated-antidepressant-medications.

33. Williams, M. T. (2018). Cultural trauma and mental health. *Journal of Clinical Psychology*; Emily Mendenhall, *Syndemic Suffering: Social Distress, Depression, and Diabetes among Mexican Immigrant Women* (Routledge, 2012).

34. Iyengar, R. (2019). *Well-intended medicine.* Stanford University Press; Angus Deaton, *The Great Escape: Health, Wealth, and the Origins of Inequality (*Princeton University Press, 2013).

35. Richard A. Friedman, "Anti-depressants' black-box warning—10 years later," *New England Journal of Medicine* 371, no. 18 (2014): 1666–1668, https://doi.org/10.1056/NEJMp1408480.

36. Steven S. Sharfstein, "Big Pharma and American Psychiatry: The Good, the Bad, and the Ugly," *Psychiatric News* 40, no. 16 (August 2005): 3–4, doi:10.1176/pn.40.16.00400003; Lydia Green, "Confessions of an Advertising Writer: How I Helped Pharma Sell Antidepressants," Mad in America, published April 2, 2025, https://www.madinamerica.com/2025/04/in-brain-chemistry-we-trust-the-gospel-according-to-pharma/; Josef Witt-Doerring, "SSRI's Are the Scam of the Century: Doctor Reacts to Matt Walsh," posted February 21, 2025, by Dr. Josef, YouTube, https://youtu.be/pCGhLiyTWMk?si=aXJhH5MOyYHEpICn.

37. Laura Clerici et al, "Gut microbiome, Diet and Depression: Literary Review of Microbiological, Nutritional and Neuroscientific Aspects," *Current Nutrition Reports* 14, no. 1 (2025): 30, https://doi.org/10.1007/s13668-025-00619-2.

38. Joanna Moncrieff, "The serotonin theory of depression."

39. K. Potter, E.J. Gayle, and S. Deb, "Effect of gut microbiome on serotonin metabolism: a personalized treatment approach" *Naunyn-Schmiedeberg's Arch Pharmacol* 397, no. 5 (2024): 2589–2602 , https://doi.org/10.1007/s00210-023-02762-5.

40. Potter, Gayle, and Deb, "Effect of gut microbiome."

41. "Ketamine," Drug Fact Sheet, U.S. Drug Enforcement Administration, updated December 2024, https://www.dea.gov/sites/default/files/2025-01/Ketamine-Drug-Fact-Sheet.pdf.

42. Elizabeth D. Ballard and Carlos A. Zarate, "The role of dissociation in ketamine's antidepressant effects," *Nature Communications* 11, no. 6431 (2020), https://doi.org/10.1038/s41467-020-20190-4.

43. Robin L. Carhart-Harris et al., "Psilocybin with psychological support for treatment-resistant depression: An open-label feasibility study," *The Lancet Psychiatry* 3, no. 7 (July 2016): 619–627, https://doi.org/10.1016/S2215-0366(16)30065-7.

44. Robin L. Carhart-Harris et al., "Trial of psilocybin versus escitalopram for depression," *The New England Journal of Medicine* 384, no. 15 (April 2021): 1402–1411, https://doi.org/10.1056/NEJMoa2032994.

45. Ricardo Evens, Marianna Elisa Schmidt, Tomislav Majic, and Timo Torsten Schmidt, "The psychedelic afterglow phenomenon: a systematic review of subacute effects of classic serotonergic psychedelics," *Therapeutic Advances in Psychopharmacology* 13 (2023): 20451253231172254, https://doi.org/10.1177/20451253231172254.

46. Richard G. Tedeschi and Lawrence G. Calhoun, *Trauma and Transformation: Growing in the Aftermath of Suffering* (Sage Publications, 1995); Richard G. Tedeschi and Lawrence G. Calhoun, "The Posttraumatic Growth Inventory: Measuring the Positive Legacy of Trauma," *Journal of Traumatic Stress* 9, no. 3 (1996): 455–471, https://doi.org/10.1002/jts.2490090305; H. Magne, N. Jaafari, and M. Voyer, "La croissance post-traumatique : un concept méconnu de la psychiatrie françaisePost-traumatic growth: Some conceptual considerations," *L'Encephale* 47, no. 2 (2021): 143–150, https://doi.org/10.1016/j.encep.2020.05.021.

47. Richard G. Tedeschi, Jane Shakespeare-Finch, and Kanako Taku, *Posttraumatic Growth: Theory, Research, and Applications* (Routledge 2018), https://doi.org/10.4324/9781315527451.

48. Pim Cuijpers, Tara Donker, Myrna M. Weissman, Paula Ravitz, and Ioana A. Cristea, "Interpersonal Psychotherapy for Mental Health Problems: A Comprehensive Meta-Analysis," *American Journal of Psychiatry* 173, no. 7 (July 2016): 680–87. doi:10.1176/appi.ajp.2015.15091141.

49. Liliana Dell'Osso et al., "Post Traumatic Growth (PTG) in the Frame of Traumatic Experiences," *Clinical Neuropsychiatry* 19, no. 6 December 2022): 390–393, https://doi.org/10.36131/cnfioritieditore20220606.

50. Pim Cuijpers et al., "Cognitive Behavior Therapy for Mental Disorders in Adults: A Unified Series of Meta-Analyses," *JAMA Psychiatry* 82, no. 6 (June 2025): 563–571, https://doi.org/10.1001/jamapsychiatry.2025.0482.

51. Mia Skytte O'Toole et al., "Cognitive behavioral therapies are evidence-based – based on what? A systematic review and meta-analysis of recent randomized controlled trials of cognitive behavioral therapies for depression," *Journ*al *of Affective Disorders* 390 (December 2025), https://doi.org/10.1016/j.jad.2025.119791.

52. Bassam Khoury et al., "Mindfulness-based therapy: a comprehensive meta-analysis," *Clinical Psychology Review* 33, no. 6 (August 2013): 763–771, https://doi.org/10.1016/j.cpr.2013.05.005.

53. A.T. Gloster et al., "The empirical status of acceptance and commitment therapy: a review of meta-analyses," *Journal of Contextual Behavioral Science* 18 (2020): 181–192, https://doi.org/10.1016/j.jcbs.2020.09.009.

54. Pim Cuijpers, "Cognitive Behavior Therapy for Mental Disorders in Adults."

55. Dennis Ougrin, "Efficacy of exposure versus cognitive therapy in anxiety disorders: system review and meta-analysis," *BMC Psychiatry* 11 (December 2011): 200, https://doi.org/10.1186/1471-244x-11-200.

56. Shizhen Wang et al., "Effectiveness of mindfulness-based cognitive therapy via e-health on anxiety and depression in adults: a meta-analysis," *General Hospital Psychiatry* 96 (Sept-Oct 2025): 211–222, https://doi.org/10.1016/j.genhosppsych.2025.07.017.

57. Pedro Rasines-Laudes and Isabel Serrano-Pintado, "Efficacy of EMDR in post-traumatic stress disorder: a systemic review and meta-analysis of randomized clinical trials," *Psicothema* 35, no. 4 (2023): 385–396, https://www.psicothema.com/pdf/4820.pdf.

58. Gordon J.G. Asmundson et al., "A meta-analytic review of cognitive processing therapy for adults with posttraumatic stress disorder," *Cognitive Behaviour Therapy* 48, no. 1 (2019): 1–14, https://doi.org/10.1080/16506073.2018.1522371.

59. Murat Genç and Ozden Y. Alkar, "The effectiveness of nature-based interventions in combating PTSD: a meta-analysis and systematic review," *Journal of Environmental Psychology* 104, 102627 (June 2025), https://doi.org/10.1016/j.jenvp.2025.102627.

60. Milton Hernandez-Bustamante et al., "Efficacy of Dialetical Behavior Therapy in the Treatment of Borderline Personality Disorder: A Systematic Review of Randomized Controlled Trials," *Iranian Journal of Psychiatry* 19, no. 1 (2024): 119–129, https://doi.org/10.18502/ijps.v19i1.14347.

61. R. Schwenker, C.E. Dietrich, S. Hirpa, M. Nothacker, G. Smedslund, T. Frese, and S. Unverzagt, "Motivational interviewing for substance use reduction," *Cochrane Database of Systematic Reviews* 12, no. CD008063 (2023), https://doi.org/10.1002/14651858.CD008063.pub3.

62. Rebecca Kim, "Addressing the Lack of Diversity in the Mental Health Field," National Alliance on Mental Illness, posted March 7, 2022, https://

www.nami.org/blog/addressing-the-lack-of-diversity-in-the-mental-health-field/.

63. Anita Henderson et al., "Personal trauma history and secondary traumatic stress in mental health professionals: a systematic review," *Journal of Psychiatric and Mental Health Nursing* 32, no. 1 (2025): 13–30, https://doi.org/10.1111/jpm.13082.

64. Frankl, *Man's Search for Meaning.*

65. Andrea Gibson, *Take Me with You* (Plume, 2018).

66. Meggan Watterson, *Mary Magdalene Revealed: The First Apostle, Her Feminist Gospel & the Christianityy We Haven't Tried Yet (*Hay House, 2021).

67. Ryan, *Soul Work.*

68. Parker J. Palmer, Arthur Zajonc, and Megan Scribner, *The Heart of Higher Education: A Call to Renewl* (Jossey-Bass, 2010).

69. Stanislav Grof, *Beyond the Brain: Birth, Death, and Transcendence in Psychotherapy* (SUNY Press, 1985); Abraham H. Maslow, "The farther reaches of human nature," *Journal of Transpersonal Psychology* 1, no. 1 (1969): 1–9.

70. "The Emerald Tablet of Hermes," Sacred-Texts.com, accessed May 11, 2026, https://sacred-texts.com/alc/emerald.htm.

71. Ram Dass, "Become Impeccable," audio recording from August 1989, posted to *Here and Now* podcast, episode 128, May 16, 2018, hosted by Raghu Markus, https://beherenownetwork.com/ram-dass-here-and-now-ep-128-become-impeccable/.

72. Benjamin Franklin, *The Autobiography of Benjamin Franklin* (Yale University Press, 1989).

73. Rachel Yehuda and Linda M. Bierer, "The relevance of epigenetics to PTSD: impliation for the DSM-V'" *Journal of Traumatic Stress* 22, no. 5 (2009): 427–434, https://doi.org/10.1002/jts.20448.

74. Dacher Keltner and Jonathan Haidt, "Approaching awe, a moral, spiritual, and aesthetic emotion," *Cognition and Emotion* 17, no. 2 (2003): 297–314, https://doi.org/10.1080/02699930302297.

75. "2024 National Survey on Drug Use and Health (NSDUH) Releases," Substance Abuse and Mental Health Services Administration, last updated September 8, 2025, https://www.samhsa.gov/data/data-we-collect/nsduh-national-survey-drug-use-and-health/national-releases/2024.

76. Carl G. Jung, *Memories, Dreams, Reflections,* ed. A. Jaffé, trans. R. Winston and C. Winston (Vintage Books, 1989).

About the Author

Tiffany Ryan, MSW, PhD, LMT, is a writer, educator, and speaker working at the intersection of mental health, meaning, and social systems of care. Trained as a social worker, her work draws on critical social work traditions, lived experience, and years of teaching to examine how people navigate what she describes as the Human Experience Labyrinth—the complex, nonlinear terrain of suffering, identity, care, and belonging.

Rather than framing distress as pathology to be corrected, Dr. Ryan has developed a post pathology framework that understands mental health as a process of orientation and reorientation within this labyrinth. Her work centers meaning, relational context, and agency. It does not seek to replace mental health treatment, but to expand how individuals and institutions understand what it means to move through crisis, diagnosis, and care while embracing humanity and meaning-centered growth.

Dr. Ryan offers educational talks, trainings, and consultation for institutions and practitioners seeking to move beyond reductionist models. She offers limited 1:1 transformation work for those focused on personal expansion, and for helpers and leaders seeking to create a ripple effect for their organizations and communities.

She is also the author of *Noah Grants Hope: 231 Days of a Mother's Transformation* and *Soul Work: A Field Guide to Freedom.*

You can connect with Dr. Ryan at www.drtiffanyryan.org.

www.ingramcontent.com/pod-product-compliance
Lightning Source LLC
Chambersburg PA
CBHW031346230926
51848CB00002B/406
* 9 7 8 1 9 6 0 8 9 2 7 6 8 *